# TEACHING READING:
*A Handbook*

**Lawrence W. Carrillo**

*St. Martin's Press*
New York

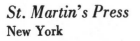

*To my mother,
who just published her
first book
at the age of seventy-nine*

# PREFACE

More has been written about the teaching of reading than about any other area of education. There are thousands of research studies, hundreds of tests, and scores of professional books. Teaching materials are available in dozens of forms and for all levels of instruction. Professional books and journals overflow with suggestions for activities to employ, games to construct, and approaches to use. Even the introductory textbooks often seem to contain more information than anyone could possibly assimilate or use. It is small wonder that teachers, and especially teachers-to-be, are often confused and intimidated by the wealth of material available to them.

*Teaching Reading: A Handbook* is intended to serve as a kind of map through this embarrassment of riches. It summarizes the basic concerns and approaches in the teaching of reading. In addition, it supplies extensive reference lists for further study of particular topics, a glossary of professional terminology, and descriptions and evaluations of available materials. Obviously, in a book so brief, I have not attempted to tell all there is to know about the topics discussed. Rather, I have tried to provide clear, concise overviews of methods and materials that can serve as introductory or supplementary reading for the student and as a reference tool for the experienced classroom or remedial teacher. This is true *handbook*, with the emphasis on practical ideas and information for teachers.

It is my hope that *Teaching Reading: A Handbook* will help teachers to teach that most basic and important of skills—reading—more enjoyably and effectively.

L.W.C.

# CONTENTS

# TEACHING READING:
## *A Handbook*

# 1 **READING AND ITS DEVELOPMENT**

For most people interested in reading instruction, it is surprising to find, upon first entering the field, the wide range of opinion on what reading is, whether or not it is an essential skill, and how it develops. Though this book is meant to be a compendium of approaches to reading instruction, it does present a definite viewpoint on what is involved in reading, why it is an important skill, and how it can be developed in others. This chapter will present these fundamentals, and the remainder of the book will explore the range of techniques available for implementing such principles.

## A DEFINITION OF READING

Reading is not something that happens to you automatically when you arrive at a certain chronological age. Given the correct environment, reading may be acquired at many stages of growth and development. If either the ability to achieve a skill of this complexity or the proper teaching is lacking, reading skill will not occur. (Even though some very bright children "teach themselves" to read, they must have some assistance from those who already read.)

Perhaps the word "skill" is misleading. Reading is actually a cohesive *set* of skills that must be carefully presented in an orderly sequence to be efficiently used then and later. The most important ingredients, then, are the teacher and the teaching.

But, in developing reading skills, what must teachers teach? Opinions among educators and psychologists differ as to what should be included in the definition of reading. These opinions may be broadly summarized in three categories:

*1. Reading is purely a mechanical process.* Advocates of this narrow view mark progress in reading skill by (a) a reader's accuracy in recognizing words and in attacking words that are not known; (b) the amount of print recognized at each fixation of the eyes; (c) the rate of recognition of words and phrases; and (d) rhythmic progress along the line of print and an easy return sweep to the next line.

*2. Reading is a mechanical process plus the acquisition of meaning.* Advocates of this broader view hold that in addition to acquiring efficiency in the mechanical aspects given above, the reader must fuse the meanings represented by the printed words into a chain of related ideas.

*3. Reading is a combination of mechanics, understanding, retention, and use.* In this broadest of the three views, the reader should be able not only to perform the mechanics and comprehend the meanings of the words, but to critically evaluate the ideas expressed and apply them to his or her situation.

Of the three views expressed, the last is closest to the philosophy of this book. That is not to say that all of the processes mentioned will be present from the earliest stages of reading. On the contrary, growth in reading skills and personal growth go hand in hand. The other two views of reading are weak because they do not recognize this maturation process. They are insufficient in other respects as well.

The first view is insufficient because, clearly, reading is *not* merely a simple mechanical process of eye movements, fixations, and return sweeps to the next line. Eye movements are only symptoms of what is happening to the reader—the overt actions that accompany the process of visual perception. In fact, they are not even necessary for reading to occur. In reading braille, for example, there are no eye movements, but the process is still reading. Thus, mastering the "mechanics" of reading is not enough. Any contrivance designed to teach only the mechanical aspects of reading is doing only a small portion of the job.

Nor is reading simply the recognition of words in printed form and the ability to "call" these words orally. It is possible to say printed words orally, or even recognize them silently, and still obtain nothing from the page. Most good readers have had the experience of "calling" the words without gaining the ideas. Production of the sound of the symbols on the printed page does not ensure that the meaning of those symbols is obtained. Recognition of each word does not necessarily convey the thoughts intended. Any approach that stops with the pronouncing of the words stops short.

The second view, though it sounds more convincing than the first, also errs by simplification. Reading is not deriving meaning from print because there are no real meanings in print, only symbols that stand for meanings. Each of the words on a page will have meanings that are somewhat specific to the writer, since they are based on his or her particular experiences. But, when readers perceive these symbols, they will recall their *own* experiences associated with the same symbols. Consequently, the meaning obtained from a page derives from readers' experiential backgrounds and is not likely to be identical with the writer's intent. To put it simply, when we read we *give* meaning to the print; we do not *take* meaning from it.

The critique has shown what reading is not, but it has also given specific clues as to what reading is. An adequate definition would say that reading is:

Thinking, with print as the stimulus

The reorganization of our own experiential background

Reacting in a variety of ways determined by the experiences of the writer, but perceived through the experience of the reader

A process that should lead to a modification of thought and 'or behavior by using the concepts developed in the process

For more complete discussions defining reading, see:

Clymer, Theodore. "What Is Reading: Some Current Concepts," in Helen M. Robinson, ed., *Innovation and Change in Reading Instruction*. Sixty-seventh Yearbook of the National Society for the Study of Education, Part II. Chicago: University of Chicago Press, 1968.

Dallmann, Martha, et al. *The Teaching of Reading*. 4th ed. New York: Holt, Rinehart & Winston, 1974. (Chapter 1 and 2.)

Gray, William S. "The Major Aspects of Reading," in Helen M. Robinson, ed., *Sequential Development of Reading Abilities*. Supplementary Educational Monographs, No. 90. Chicago: University of Chicago Press, 1960.

## WHY TEACH READING?

Reading as an important means of communication has its detractors today who claim it is not competitive with other modes. Where there used to be a bookcase, there is now a television set. Our ears are bombarded by audio-approaches—music, speeches, or sometimes just plain noises. The transistor radio may be found far back in the African "bush." But it is not so much a question of which is the best means of communication, but rather which means is best for each purpose, each situation, and each person.

There are values (even for better reading) in various media. Librarians know of the sudden demand for a book when the movie based on that book is playing in town. Television is increasing the vocabulary and broadening the vicarious experiences of children. Radio may have contributed more to a standardized pronunciation of American English than all of the schools.

But when reading skills have been developed, people have available to them the collected knowledge and pleasure the human race has been able to achieve. Those who read well silently can cover a factual article in less than half the time it would take them to hear a lecture given the same information. They are also more likely to comprehend since they can govern the pace of presentation, speeding up, slowing down, or repeating according to their individual needs. Or, if the ideas are a bit "thin," they can skim over much of the verbiage to get what is there. Even with present experiments in speeded-up tape, the speed cannot approach that of good readers. And, since understanding is the desired result, individual pacing is the key to individual understanding.

It seems probable that careful instruction in reading promotes the ability to think clearly. The skills taught in the area of reading comprehension are thinking skills, and by using the printed page as a vehicle, practice in these thinking skills is provided.

Reading can also contribute to the leisure of life. Horizons are expanded and international and interpersonal understandings are promoted without traveling farther than the library. In addition, unlike actual travel that involves attention to time schedules, monetary exchanges, or taxes, "traveling" via books involves little more than picking them up at one's convenience. In short, books adapt to individuals, not the reverse.

So, reading about a subject is usually more *efficient* than listening to an oral presentation, both in terms of time spent and of understanding achieved. Moreover, even at present prices, the variety and range of topics in print is greater for the money than in any other media. Reading, thus, is still the most flexible, economical, and varied means of total communication we have at our disposal.

More complete information on the usefulness of reading can be found in:

Allen, James F., Jr. "The Right to Read: Education's New National Priority," in Sam Leaton Sebesta and Carl J. Wallen, eds., *The First R: Readings on Teaching Reading*. Chicago: Science Research Associates, 1972.
Durkin, Dolores. *Teaching Them to Read*. Boston: Allyn & Bacon, 1970.

## READING STAGES AND READING GROWTH

### Developmental Philosophy

Various aspects of children's development—their physical growth, mental maturity, emotional stability, social adjustment, and the educational situation in which they find themselves—are related to and contribute to their development in reading.

Learning to read involves the total growth and development of individuals. Accelerated or delayed progress in any area presents special problems in learning to read. Reading progress is not dictated by a calendar, but by what has gone before in the life and education of pupils. A developmental reading program is a sequential instructional plan. This plan gradually reinforces and extends reading skills, appreciations, and understandings acquired in previous years and develops new and more complex skills, appreciations, and understandings.

However, even though a basic course of study in reading may have as its foundation how typical children in our society develop, wide differences among children guarantee that we cannot successfully use such a single-track approach with such a varied population. Grade-level limits must disappear and some attention to the *individual's* sequence of development must be given before a truly successful job of teaching reading is possible. Instruction begins at each learner's current stage and leads onward to whatever rate is possible. Reading must be taught as a process, not as a subject.

### The Cone of Reading Development

Reading as a process involves several specific skills, as the "cone" of reading development on the next page shows. The cone does not come to a point at the top, indicating that further growth is always possible with some individuals. The specific skills included in each stage represent the particular teaching-learning process at that stage. (Others could be included at each level.) The left-hand side of the cone shows the five developmental stages of reading acquisition. These stages, of course, blend slightly into one another rather than being as sharply differentiated as shown. But there are distinctions, as a brief discussion of each will make clear.[1]

**Stage 1: Development of readiness for beginning reading.**  The process of learning to read starts from the moment of conception. Maturation and learning from experience contribute to the development of this process. Family and neighborhood experiences are reflected in a child's development and later school behavior.

Variations in health and nutrition may influence the learning situation, as well as such things as vision and hearing. A strong background of acquiring information and being able to profit from experience contributes to ease in learning. Strong negative emotion, if present, disorganizes and impairs the functioning of the child in learning. An ability to work with others and, when necessary, to function independently provide a necessary learning foundation. A school situation which is acceptable to the individual and his or her parents and which supplies the necessary good teaching, materials, and environment makes learning more easily possible.

Note that each of the stages of the cone is a readiness step for the succeeding stage. The schools must be concerned with readiness before beginning reading and before each successive step in reading growth. Materials and approaches are quite informal at first but gradually become more formal as the child progresses. Readiness, when achieved, results in the ability to profit from instruction at each level of a developmental sequence.

[1] The distinctions are based on those found in *Report of the National Committee on Reading*, in Twenty-fourth Yearbook of the National Society for the Study of Education, Part I (Chicago: University of Chicago Press, 1925); and Ruth Strang, Constance M. McCullough, and Arthur Traxler, *The Improvement of Reading*, 4th ed. (New York: McGraw-Hill, 1967).

**5. REFINEMENT**

Development of flexibility of rate. Refinement of comprehension (emphasis on drawing conclusions, tone and mood, inferences, critical thinking and application). Learning prefixes, suffixes, multiple word meanings, technical vocabulary. Improving study skills, interests, and tastes.

**4. WIDE READING**

Locating and using references. Continuing improvement in rate of silent reading. Rapid growth in enjoyment of print. Expansion of vocabulary, comprehension skills (emphasis, main idea, sequence). Selection, evaluation, and organization of study-type materials. Review of phonic and structural analysis (extension to syllabication and accent). Large amount of independent reading.

**3. RAPID DEVELOPMENT**

Extension of sight vocabulary and word-analysis skills (including phonic and structural analysis, use of context clues). Start of work-type skills such as use of different parts of books and selective reading to locate information. Completion of major portion of phonic analysis, including vowels, digraphs, diphthongs, and variants. Beginnings of wider reading and content-field reading. Development of the ability to read more rapidly silently, but with fluency and ease in oral reading at the same time. True recreational reading begins for most children.

**2. INITIAL READING**

Continued development of auditory and visual perception, handling of books, listening to and using language better, concept and background improvement. Beginning of a sight vocabulary of instantly recognizable words for immediate reading and for building word-attack skills; learning letter names, auditory-visual perception of consonants, consonant blends and digraphs, double consonants, and phonograms; using context and picture clues to check meaning; reading aloud for variatoin in pitch, stress, and volume; indication of relationship between speech and print; using library; learning structural elements such as inflectional variants and plurals.

**1. READINESS**

Guided development of such basics as left-right progression and top-bottom approach to printed page; differentiation of colors; visual and auditory discrimination as preparation for both sight and sound attack on words; development of fuller verbal expression; listening skills; eye, hand, and motor coordination; awareness of words and their functions; following directions; understanding of story sequence. Aided adjustment to school by building positive experiences with books, by broadening concepts, and by increasing breadth and depth of experiential background.

| Physical Development | Mental Maturity | Emotional Stability | Social Adjustment | Educational Situation |
|---|---|---|---|---|

All aspects of heredity and environment, family, and neighborhood

For further reference, see:

Carrillo, Lawrence W. *Informal Reading Readiness Experiences.* Rev. ed. New York: Noble and Noble, 1971.
Monroe, Marion, and Rogers, Bernice. *Foundations for Reading.* Chicago: Scott, Foresman, 1964.

**Stage 2: Initial stage in learning to read.** The beginnings of reading instruction are crucial. At this stage, although much of the reading is oral (with the child moving from the familiar spoken word to the unfamiliar printed word), silent reading is introduced and stress is placed on the meaning of the printed forms. Experience stories, charts, readers, flash cards, filmstrips, films, and records may be used as well as multilevel materials of some kind (trade books, multiple readers, or reading laboratory materials). The emphasis is on building a basic sight vocabulary, developing confidence in the reading situation, and beginning instruction in the word-attack skills.

Failure at this stage and the inability to progress further is likely to result either because the presentation of work is too difficult for the individual's present state of development or because too much pressure is applied for immediate achievement. A slower, more careful, broader beginning is likely to repay doubly later on in the program.

Hundreds of professional references might be suggested for further reading on this stage. For a clear and uncomplicated reference, try:

Miller, Wilma H. *The First R: Elementary Reading Today.* New York: Holt, Rinehart & Winston, 1972.

**Stage 3: Rapid development of reading skills.** Normally this stage represents the instructional program planned for the second- and third-grade books of a basal reader series. A thorough grounding in basic reading habits and skills must be provided. Major emphases are on the extension of the sight vocabulary, improvement of reading comprehension, building competence in independent word analysis (including phonetic and structural analysis, the use of context, and other clues), building interest in reading, and encouraging the beginnings of wider reading in varied source materials.

Many children in grades four through eight remain at this stage of reading development. Such retardation is not necessarily the result of poor teaching, but good teaching is necessary for remediation since such children are likely to grow and develop in many other aspects while standing still in reading. (The "teachable moment" has passed.)

In general, the same materials are used at this stage as in the previous stages, but more emphasis is placed on chalkboard work, on printed or duplicated materials, and on other types of reading materials such as supplementary readers, literary readers, or multilevel materials.

For further reference, see:

Ekwall, Eldon E. *Locating and Correcting Reading Difficulties*. Columbus, Ohio: Charles E. Merrill, 1970.
Hafner, Lawrence E., and Jolly, Hayden B. *Patterns of Teaching Reading in the Elementary School*. New York: Macmillan, 1972.

**Stage 4: Wide reading stage.**    Normally this is the reading program planned for those who are progressing well in the fourth, fifth and sixth grades. The program emphasizes continuing expansion of vocabulary (especially into areas associated with content fields), building further comprehension skills, and reviewing and adding to word-attack skills. Silent reading receives much more class time than oral reading, and the speed of silent reading begins to increase, though without a great deal of formal attention to speed. A large amount of independent reading is in order both for pleasure and for information. Because the emphasis is on independent reading, and because the increased demand for reading in content subjects at this level leaves less time for actual reading instruction, individualized, personalized, or multilevel methods of instruction assume major importance.

In general, up to this point in reading development the program has tended to be rather structured and careful, perhaps limited to a progression through one or two sets of basal readers. Thereafter, it may have a tendency to spread out in all directions. Though some variety and extension of the program is needed, and though some literary, independent, and personal aspects are essential, structure should not be neglected.

No matter which materials and methods are used at this level, there must be a constant review and reteaching of the skills as well as the addition of newer and more refined skills. Most teachers are not equipped to do this job without basing their reading program on a carefully planned basal series to which variety and individualization may then appropriately be added.

For more information, see:

Bamman, Henry A., Dawson, Mildred A., and McGovern, James J. *Fundamentals of Basic Reading Instruction*. 3rd ed. New York: David McKay, 1973.
Dallmann, Martha, et al. *The Teaching of Reading*. 4th ed. New York: Holt, Rinehart & Winston, 1974.

**Stage 5: Refinement of reading.**    Above the sixth grade of reading competence (and probably continuing through college), the reading program should still be continued. This need is now beginning to be recognized in secondary schools. Even colleges and universities have offered reading programs with developmental as well as reading aspects.

Materials used are varied and not always well directed toward the objectives stated in the curriculum. The amount of reading *required* at this stage increases, and the time for voluntary reading tends to diminish.

Much of the responsibility for the teaching of reading at this stage rests with the teachers of the content areas. *It cannot be accomplished otherwise.* The content-area teacher is, therefore, the student's last resort for the presentation and "setting" of the skills in the last two levels of the cone of reading development.

For recent writings on reading in the secondary school, see:

Aukerman, Robert C. *Reading in the Secondary School Classroom.* New York: McGraw-Hill, 1972.

Duggins, James. *Teaching Reading for Human Values in High School.* Columbus, Ohio: Charles E. Merrill, 1972.

**Progress through the cone.** Obviously, through all of these stages there is no real uniformity of progress. Though Stage 4 will be the level of the majority of intermediate-grade students, it will not be true for all. Some will be far advanced and well into Stage 5 while others will be stalled back in Stages 2 and 3. This is not usually an indication of the inadequacy of the program. The best program, in fact, will produce increased rather than decreased variability. Lags are often merely the academic symptoms of individual differences.

Individuals develop at different rates in all aspects of growth, reading growth included. Developmental reading is a series of steps, arranged in levels of increasing complexity. The stages described above are arrived at through a knowledge of child development and through what is known about the reading process.

Learning to read requires daily, systematic instruction. To move on to the next level of reading, pupils need the help of the teacher. Instruction in developmental reading is a sequence of teaching-learning situations on a gradually increasing level of complexity, governed by the developing abilities of the individual. Growth in reading skill cannot be expected if a step in the sequence of skills is omitted or if the approach is above the level of the pupil.

### Objectives of Reading Instruction

Many of the specific objectives of the reading program can be found in the cone of reading development just presented. It is also possible to find rather complete lists in many reading courses of study developed by various districts or in sources such as *The Improvement of Reading.*[2] For convenience it is useful to think of three general objectives to reading instruction, each of which includes several more specific aims.

[2] Strang, McCullough, and Traxler, *ibid.,* pp. 132–42.

The first general objective is to develop habits of intelligent and useful interpretation. Teachers can implement this objective by helping students extend their vocabulary and effective use of the language, increase their ability to communicate (through the medium of oral reading), and improve their use of the library and reference works. With such aid, students will be better able to ascertain the viewpoints of others. By exercising that ability they can keep informed of current events and practices, thereby becoming more effective citizens. And they can better plan for their future, advance in their chosen field of work, and keep abreast of developments in other fields as well.

Related to this, a second objective of reading instruction is to build new channels of interest and more refined tastes. What reading teachers select should stimulate student thinking. As a direct result of their heightened awareness, students should be able to critically evaluate printed matter and develop a broad outlook on life. They should also be able to find pleasure and recreation during their leisure time.

A third, very general objective to teaching reading is to ensure efficiency in communication through print. Teachers should strive to develop a flexible rate of comprehension in students and to increase their ability to understand all types of printed matter. Learning these skills will enable students to determine rapidly the important portions of correspondence, messages, instructions, and other written communications they will meet later in life.

In order to attain even the most mechanical of these objectives. the reading program must provide specific activities and exercises. They will help develop the skills of:

Getting the main idea of a passage or selection
Noting relevant details
Establishing sequence and organization
Predicting outcomes or solutions
Following directions
Gaining verbal images from descriptive passages
Seeing relationships within a passage or between differing sources
Drawing inferences about the writer's purpose
Determining tone and mood
Summarizing
Recognizing and interpreting literary devices
Inferring answers or details not directly stated
Evaluating facts or reasoning, determining the truth of statements
Distinguishing the relevant from the irrelevant
Making comparisons
Recognizing propaganda devices
Exchanging interpretations and coming to a common viewpoint
Building vocabulary, both general and technical
Such a complex array of skills cannot be developed during one year of

school or in one subject area of the curriculum; nor can it be assimilated totally during the elementary grades. A good series of readers will help ensure attention to the array of specifics, but it is essential that content-area books be used also. Well-established coordination and continuity among the various levels of schools in a district and among the various subject teachers is obviously necessary, as is the need for a variety of approaches and materials.

Where the teaching approach has changed from one of utilizing basal readers to an individualized approach utilizing a wide variety of materials, problems are likely to develop when it comes to ensuring the teaching and review of such an impressive array of skill objectives. This may be one of the reasons that "criterion-referenced testing" and accompanying planned materials are gaining popularity very rapidly. Some of these planned programs may be based on hundreds of specific objectives. For example, the Wisconsin Design works toward forty-five specific objectives in the area of word-attack alone.[3] For teaching these objectives, a great number of resource materials from many publishers is suggested. The *Prescriptive Reading Inventory* utilizes ninety different objectives, but many of these are repeated at several levels with increasing complexity, so that, in effect, there are perhaps two hundred specific objectives. Suggested activities for teaching each objective are listed in the *Interpretive Handbook*.[4]

Many school districts are developing their own lists of behavioral objectives for the reading program. Some are developing reading tests based on these objectives; a few are going even further by suggesting teaching methods based on the criterion objectives. Ordinarily, however, the major differences in the lists (if carefully done) are the amount of specificity in the objectives and the variety of materials available for teaching and review. Such detailed curriculum development entails a tremendous amount of work. Anyone attempting such a task should first investigate the detailed objectives (even if not behaviorally phrased) found in all the major basal reader series and then check such sources as those cited in the previous paragraph. These will, at the worst, save time; at the best, they will do the job themselves.

For beginning reading activities based on behavioral objectives, see:

Spache, Evelyn B. *Reading Activities for Child Involvement*. Boston: Allyn & Bacon, 1972.

For complete listings in both general and specific areas of reading, see:

Otto, Wayne, et al. *Focused Reading Instruction*. Reading, Mass.: Addison-Wesley, 1974.

[3] The outline of skills and behavioral objectives may be located in Appendices A and B of Wayne Otto and E. Askov, *Rationale and Guidelines; The Wisconsin Design for Reading Skill Development* (Minneapolis: National Computer Systems, 1972).

[4] *Prescriptive Reading Inventory* and *Interpretive Handbook: Prescriptive Reading Inventory* (Monterey, Calif.: CTB/McGraw-Hill, 1972).

# POPULATION CHARACTERISTICS IN READING

## *Individual Differences*

First-year teachers are often startled by the range of reading ability they find in their classes. Teachers with wide experience know that this is normal and that the better the prior teachers, the wider that range will be. Each of us differs in all things to some degree. We differ in academic aptitude, in physical growth, in emotional development, in socioeconomic background, in experience, in interests.

Research has produced averages. We have charts of height and weight norms, tables of achievement norms on tests in all subjects, and statements of developmental tasks appropriate to various age levels. However, our problem is the range on either side of the average figure. *There are not many truly average students.* Our age-grade norms give us the achievement score expected for the center of the school-age population, but almost everyone in the group will be above or below the norm—sometimes a considerable distance above or below.

Textbooks designed for specific grade levels tend to be paced in content, interest, and difficulty for the average. But as people develop and learn, they grow away from one another; they become increasingly different. Brighter children in the academic area improve much more rapidly, perhaps gaining two years with each year spent in school, while the slower children are sometimes doing quite well to gain a half year with each school year.

The following points about reading achievement are pertinent to teaching in the content areas as well as in the teaching of reading itself:

1. The range of reading levels found gradually increases from year to year. The range ordinarily will broaden between one and two years with each year in school. Specifically, at seventh grade the range will be from about third-grade level to at least tenth-grade level; at ninth grade the range will extend from high third to about twelfth in reading ability.[5]

2. The middle half (50 percent) of the children take up about one-third of the range. For example, at seventh-grade placement, the middle 50 percent will range from about sixth-grade to eighth-grade level in reading.

3. The best pupils at any grade level are about as far above the norm for the grade as those suffering from reading difficulty are below it.

4. The number of students who attain an "average" score is quite small, since the total population is spread out so far.

5. There is a great deal of overlapping of levels of reading skill from grade to grade. In general, the next higher grade is not greatly different from the one preceding it.

[5] For a chart showing the range of reading expected by grades, from grades one through eight, see Lawrence W. Carrillo, *Informal Reading Readiness Experiences*, rev. ed. (New York: Noble & Noble, 1971).

6. Each teacher, therefore, is teaching many "grade levels" of reading.

In addition to the problem of range of differences, there is the problem of differing growth cycles. The graph of a student's growth in reading is never a smooth upward curve. It is rather a succession of rises, lags, plateaus, drops, and spurts. Also, a pupil may score much higher in recognition vocabulary, for example, than in comprehension. He or she may also be able to understand very well everything read but be unable to cover very much because of lack of reading speed. Any number of individual variations are possible even when the grade-equivalent score on a reading test is the same for two or more individuals. Both instruction and curriculum must be adjusted to the differences from pupil to pupil as well as to the differences in level of ability.

### *Achievement in Reading and Its Relation to Intelligence*

Reading, as stated earlier, is a process of giving meanings to printed symbols and organizing these meanings in terms of the writer's presentation. The meanings of the words are based on the reader's experiences associated with the words. Consequently, intellectual limitations make it difficult for the reader to (1) recall his or her experiences with the word, (2) apply these experiences to the abstract printed word, (3) reorganize these personal meanings in terms of the author's system, and (4) use the new system of meanings.

The intelligence test is one approach to determining the potential for reading in an individual, but there are a number of cautions in using these tests. Almost all intelligence tests require reading; if the person taking the test cannot read well, the IQ score achieved has little meaning. If, over several years, the student would normally have been expected to read but could not, he or she will also have lost some of the background normal for the present chronological age and will score lower. If he or she comes from an environment in which the usual middle-class cultural experiences are not present, the test score will also be lower. However, in spite of these and other limitations, intelligence tests are probably the best quick way of estimating reading potential, though tests of listening comprehension can and should be used.

Individually administered tests such as the Binet or the Wechsler-Bellevue will give the most accurate estimates of intellectual capacity and should be used if possible. Group pencil-and-paper tests are subject to many errors, but they do give a rough estimate of capacity that is close enough for most practical purposes.

To estimate reading potential from an intelligence test which has just been administered, first find the mental age score achieved (*not* the IQ). Then subtract five years from this figure (for the number of years of mental development before school attendance and reading instruction). The number found will be an *estimate* of the reading grade level of the child. For example:

Mental Age   =    9.5
Subtract 5.0     −5.0
                 —————
                 4.5    (Reading Grade Level Estimate)

Another approach to estimating reading potential is through listening comprehension on graded paragraphs. Paragraphs of this nature may be located in any of the individual reading tests,[6] or in the informal reading inventories developed by many districts and authorities.[7]

However, it must be emphasized that in using measures of intelligence and listening comprehension and predicting reading potential from them, the variables are so numerous that the results should always be suspect. Measured intelligence is subject to change as circumstances and opportunities change. Potential for reading instruction as evaluated by tests may be different next year, or perhaps even next month! This caution applies particularly to those children coming from different cultures and environments, but, in any case, application of this estimate calls for caution.

[6] See, for example, Robert McCracken, *Standard Reading Inventory* (Bellingham, Wash.: Pioneer Printing); and Donald D. Durrell, *Durrell Analysis of Reading Difficulty* (New York: Harcourt Brace Jovanovich, 1965).

[7] See Nila B. Smith, et al., *Graded Selections for Informal Reading Diagnosis* (New York: New York University Press, 1959, 1963); and Marjorie S. Johnson and Roy A. Kress, *Informal Reading Inventories*, Reading Aid Series. (Newark, Del.: International Reading Association, 1965).

# 2 METHODS OF TEACHING READING

This chapter discusses the most common methods used in reading instruction. In some cases the most pertinent *advantages* and *disadvantages* will be stated. Of course, any particular method may have several variations, and it is extremely rare for a "pure" method to be continued in operation in a single classroom for any period of time. Since knowledge of a variety of methods is desirable, further references are given at the conclusion of the explanation of each method.

## THE EXPERIENCE METHOD

In this approach the teacher takes advantage of the children's interests and backgrounds to produce reading material with which to teach. Children relate experiences and the teacher writes down (usually on the chalkboard as a first step) some of the things they say. Later the teacher can transfer the "experience story" to a large chart. Sentence strips and word cards can also be made for matching purposes, to use in games, or for other activities.

Usually, one child after another reads successive sentences, and then a child or two will read the entire story. It the chart is to be permanent, tagboard is usually used, but because most experience stories are not worth using many times, newsprint is best. In the primary grades, the teacher should use manuscript letters to approximate typed or printed material. A felt pen, a black or colored crayon, a nylon-tipped pen, or rubber letter-stamps can be used to form the letters, but legibility and the distance of the reader from the chart must be considered. For most group teaching, letters three-fourths of an inch to one inch high seem sufficiently large.

Among the possible advantages of this method, the most notable are:

—The vocabulary is the child's own. Meaning and understanding are already present.

—Because the stories come from the children and represent their own experiences, they are almost certain to be interesting to them.

—Important phases of comprehension, such as sequence and organization, and attention to expression, are included naturally through the medium of the pupil's experience.

—Individual differences can be accommodated rather easily.

—Reading is not formal or remote but a natural outgrowth of experience.

—Great flexibility of content is permitted.

There are, however, several disadvantages:

—Vocabulary control is difficult. If too many new words are introduced at one time, the child may learn none of them.

—The reading material developed may lose its initial interest if used many times.

—Sight vocabulary may not be repeated sufficiently often in varying contexts to ensure complete learning, and a great deal of guessing at words may result.

—Because the teacher must spend a great deal of time and effort in making the charts, he or she may not be able to spend enough time in other areas.

—Pupils tend to memorize the materials, giving them a false impression of the act of reading.

—Literary quality is not likely to be high. The content may be restricted, and the organization and sequence may be poor.

—It is often difficult to include material from all of the children in the group.

The experience method is a good approach in beginning reading and offers an easy transition to books. It can also be used as a valuable supplement to printed materials, adding interest and flexibility. When used as a "pure" method, however, the disadvantages tend rapidly to overcome the advantages, especially at stages beyond beginning reading.

For inspiration and information, see:

Allen, Roach Van, and Allen, Claryce. *Language Experiences in Reading: Teacher's Resource Book.* Chicago: Encyclopedia Britannica Press, 1966.

Ashton-Warner, Sylvia. *Teacher.* New York: Simon & Schuster, 1963.

Carrillo, Lawrence W. "The Language-Experience Approach to the Teaching of Reading," in John Downing and Amy L. Brown, eds., *The Second International Reading Symposium.* London: Cassell, 1967.

Gans, Roma. *Guiding Children's Reading Through Experiences.* New York: Bureau of Publications, Teachers College, Columbia University, 1941.

Herrick, Virgil E., and Nerbovig, Marcella. *Using Experience Charts with Children.* Columbus, Ohio: Charles E. Merrill, 1964.

Lee, Dorris M., and Allen, R. Van. *Learning to Read Through Experience.* 2nd ed. New York: Appleton-Century-Crofts, 1963.

## SIGHT, OR "LOOK AND SAY," METHODS

There are several methods of this kind with a common theoretical basis. Different names for these methods may be found, but those most often used are "the sight-word method," "the word-phrase method," and "the sentence-story method," depending upon the length of the printed unit used.

In the sight-word method, the teacher puts a word on the board or uses a chart. He or she pronounces the word, has several of the children pronounce it, and then combines it with other words to form sentences. Pictures are used to introduce words since they relate more directly to experiences than the abstract printed form. Children recognize the words first by general shape or configuration.

The sight-word method is not particularly new. John Amos Comenius, author of the first illustrated textbook (1658), not only introduced pictures as helps in learning but also formally suggested this method of teaching reading. The first American educator to recommend the sight-word method was Samuel Worcester, author of *Primer of the English Language* (1828).

Gradually other proponents of new methods suggested that there was more meaning in a phrase, a sentence, and finally a whole story than there was in the word, and that the meaningful unit should be lengthened. The word-phrase method presents an entire sentence at a time. The sentence is divided into words which are then used in many different sentences. In the story method the teacher reads a story over and over until most of the children have memorized it. The teacher then shows them the first sentences, reads the sentences aloud, and has the children say the lines as they look at them.

Each of these methods rests on the initial presentation of meaningful units. Through repeated exposure, the child learns to associate the *meaning and pronunciation* of words he can speak with the printed forms of those same words. Gradually the oral stimulus is omitted, and the sight of the symbol by itself will convey the meaning. In all respects these methods put the emphasis on meaning. The child adds new stimuli to old experiences. If we wish to give meaning to the printed form *dog*, we first talk about dogs so that the child will recall former experiences with this symbol. We say the word *dog* and he or she repeats it. Then we show a picture of a dog, if possible, and at the same time show the printed symbol—always pronouncing the word since the spoken form is known. Soon the child will extend the chain of his or her experiences to include this new stimulus and will associate the printed form with the spoken form and with previous feelings and concepts about dogs. The discovery that printed words "talk" is one of the first steps in learning to read.

In extreme sight-method situations, lists of words are used. The children are drilled on these words and are required to recognize them at sight. Flash cards merely vary the order of presentation. In this way the meaning of the word vanishes, and the advantage of the meaningful unit is lost.

Where the method is not so extreme, words are introduced gradually in context and repeated extensively. The teacher then begins to develop in students greater observation of the details and smaller features of these words. The words are learned before the names or sounds of the letters inasmuch as the letter or sound of the letter is not a meaningful unit when separated from the word.

Some of the advantages of the "look and say" method, whether used with words, phrases, sentences, or stories, are:

—Children associate meaning with their first attempts at reading; the emphasis is on comprehension.

—Appreciation of reading as an enjoyable activity may come rapidly since it does not take long to develop ability to read a simple story in which many of the words are repeated.

—Learning larger units rather than smaller units such as letters tends to make reading more rapid and adds to the speed of understanding in later stages of development when speed becomes more necessary.

—Children tend naturally to learn by larger units first, and then to learn about components of the larger units with which they are already familiar. Therefore, this type of learning is relatively easy for children.

The method also has certain limitations:

—Children do not always look at the word when it is being pronounced and therefore do not carry through the expected association.

—Adults tend to think in terms of smaller building blocks of reading and may object strenuously to the method; if this attitude is conveyed to children, they may resist this learning situation.

—A child who fails in the beginning has no method of proceeding on his own since, if this method is used exclusively, no word attack is possible in the beginning stages unless someone pronounces the word.

—If the language background of the child is different from that of others in the group and not suited to the school form of language, a long period of "language readiness" is necessary.

For more information on this method, see:

Anderson, Irving H., and Dearborn, Walter F. *The Psychology of Teaching Reading.* New York: Ronald Press, 1952.

Hafner, Lawrence E., and Jolly, Hayden B. *Patterns of Teaching Reading in the Elementary School.* New York: Macmillan, 1972.

Smith, Nila Banton. *American Reading Instruction.* Newark, Del.: International Reading Association, 1962.

Zintz, Miles V. *The Reading Process.* Dubuque, Iowa: William C. Brown, 1970.

# WORD-ATTACK METHODS

Included in this category are two methods usually called structural analysis and phonic analysis.

Structural analysis involves the recognition of new words by noting known roots, word parts, or whole words, and combining these with inflectional endings (*s* or *ed*), prefixes and suffixes, and other known words. Syllabication and accent placement are also usually considered as part of structural analysis. This approach to reading is never advanced as a full approach but always appears as supplemental to other methods such as phonics, the basal reader, or the sight method. As a matter of fact, some sight recognition of word parts (the root or common part of words) is essential in the beginning stages of structural analysis if further progress is to be possible. The inclusion of the analysis of word structure in a reading program has been shown to have real value, especially for the brighter children.

The phonic method involves associating basic speech sounds with letter symbols and their combinations in order to identify words. In the phonic method as originally conceived, the teacher started the reading program with drill on letter sounds as the first step in reading. The next procedure was to teach the child how to blend the sounds together in words that could be recognized, starting with two- or three-letter words. After drill on words incorporating the sounds was finished and the children knew some words, books and stories were introduced. Writing or tracing was (and is, in present-day phonic systems) often incorporated into the method, especially for non-phonetic words.

In general, the advantages of these "synthetic" methods (so-called because a synthesis of word parts is employed) are:

—Children rapidly develop independence in discovering for themselves what the word is.

—Oral reading and pronunciation may be improved.

—Material that is quite difficult may be given to children to read in the primary grades. (The reading, however, may be mere word calling.)

—These methods work in some cases where the visual approach does not, especially with older remedial cases.

As with the other methods, there are also disadvantages:

—Such programs are rather rigid and incorporate a larger amount of drill in the early stages. Many children will not accept these types of programs.

—There may be a lack of interest in the beginning stages because there is no true reading, only a recitation of sounds.

—There is little attention to meaning; attention is focused on sound, and comprehension tends to suffer.

—These methods are likely to produce readers who read in a slow, labored fashion, with much lip movement and vocalization.

For a more complete discussion and references, see "What About Phonics?" in the next chapter.

## THE ALPHABET-SPELLING METHOD

In this method the names of the letters are taught first. Then the letters of words are named in sequence, and finally the word is pronounced. In many languages this procedure is more effective than in English, since in English the names of the letters may have little to do with their sound: for example, *are-ay-tee* bears little relation to the pronunciation of *rat*. The method was used widely during the nineteenth century, and the preface of the McGuffey primer states that this method can be used with that book. Because of the differences between names of letters and their sounds, however, the phonic method gradually supplanted the alphabet method.

Using this method with the English language has no apparent advantages, and the disadvantages are those of other synthetic methods (phonics and structural analysis), with the added problem of the lack of correspondence between the names and sounds of letters.

For further references on the subject, see:

Burton, William, Baker, Clara, and Kemp, Grace. *Reading in Child Development.* New York: Henry Holt & Co., 1956.

Fries, Charles C. *Linguistics and Reading.* New York: Holt, Rinehart & Winston, 1962.

Smith, Frank. *Understanding Reading.* New York: Holt, Rinehart & Winston, 1971.

Strang, Ruth, and Bracken, Dorothy. *Making Better Readers.* Boston: D. C. Heath, 1957.

## THE ORAL READING METHOD

Incorporated into nearly all other methods is the oral reading approach. It can hardly be called a method in itself. It is mentioned here because of the problem of the amount of oral reading that should be included. When children are in the beginning stages, it provides an opportunity for the teacher to detect an error in reading as it occurs so that it can be corrected immediately and not repeated. Furthermore, it tends to provide the intermediate step from spoken to printed language. On the other hand, after the initial stages of reading instruction, a great deal of oral reading does not add much to the reading program, and "oral reading around the group" may become a problem rather than a help. Since about 1920 the emphasis in the reading program has progressed toward silent reading.

For a discussion of procedures and for further references, see the section entitled "Oral Reading" in the next chapter.

## THE NON-ORAL METHOD

In several articles and studies between 1937 and 1945, J. E. McDade and G. T. Buswell reported on a method of purely visual reading that omitted the spoken portion of the lesson entirely. In this method pupils are told not to say the words even to themselves. Instead, words are shown in conjunction with pictures, objects, and actions, and a period of oral preparation *precedes* the reading lesson. The oral symbol and the printed symbol are never presented together as in other methods.

The idea here was to induce a see-and-comprehend process without the intermediate step of saying, thereby overcoming the problem of vocalization. In careful experiments with this method, however, there was no significant difference, even in terms of lip movement, between groups taught in this manner and groups taught with usual methods involving oral reading. These experiments demonstrated the unimportance of the method as compared with other factors such as child development and the spread of individual differences in a school population. This point should be remembered when any "pure" method is advocated.

For a thorough discussion of the method, see:

Buswell, G. T. *Non-Oral Reading: A Study of Its Use in the Chicago Public Schools.* Supplementary Educational Monographs, No. 60. Chicago: University of Chicago Press, 1945.

McDade, J. E. *Essentials of Non-Oral Beginning Reading.* Chicago: Plymouth Press, 1941.

## THE AUDIO-VISUAL METHOD (NEW CASTLE PLAN)

In a number of articles in professional journals, Glenn McCracken has presented results of experiments in New Castle, Pennsylvania, using a somewhat different method. His method uses colored filmstrips developed for use with a basal reader series. The content of the filmstrips is parallel to but not identical with the content of the series. All initial instruction for each lesson is given in the filmstrip, and projected images of the reading material are used. The texts themselves serve as testing and practice material. Data presented show extremely favorable results, although some authorities question the controls used and the amount of time spent in this program in comparison with others.

The advantages would seem to be:

1. Students maintain high interest and attention.

2. There is careful preparation for every lesson through use of the filmstrips.

3. The large colored projection is vivid, the room is semidark, and there are few things to distract the attention of the pupils.

4.   The size of print may be better adapted to farsighted young pupils than is the print in books.

5.   When the text is projected on the chalkboard, the group can work together on the exact materials, whereas underlining or other forms of marking in the book are usually frowned upon.

There are, however, some possible disadvantages:

1.   Since the lessons are "canned," the creative teacher has little opportunity to do special things for her or his group to accommodate their particular needs.

2.   The transfer to the printed page may present some problems.

3.   Use of a wider variety of materials is not as likely because of the time spent with this approach and the dearth of adapted materials.

4.   Utilization of practices such as grouping and other adaptations to individual differences is difficult.

For further reference, see:

McCracken, Glenn. "New Castle Reading Experiment: A Terminal Report." *Elementary English* 30 (1953), 13–21.
———. "The Value of the Correlated Visual Image." *The Reading Teacher* 13 (1959), 29–33.

## THE KINESTHETIC METHOD

In 1921 Grace Fernald described a technique that has been used with much success, especially in remedial reading. In the early stages children are asked to tell a few words they would like to learn and these are taught one by one. The method of teaching words changes as they improve and occurs in four stages.

The first stage, which gives the method its name, requires the physical involvement of the children in tracing. The word is written or printed on strips of paper (4 x 10 inches) and the children trace it with their fingers, saying each part of the word as they trace it. They practice until they can write it from memory, testing themselves on a scrap of paper and checking their work with the original. In order to fix the word, they then use it in a story they are asked to compose. Each new word learned is placed in an alphabetical file which every child keeps. Finger contact with the paper is considered very important. The children never copy a word but rather write from memory and then compare the result with their model. The word is always written as a whole. Pronunciation by parts must always accompany the tracing, and transfer is provided by the teacher's typing whatever the children have written.

After a while the children do not need to trace all words. At this second stage they look at the word, say it to themselves several times, and write it from memory. Cards are substituted for the strips but are still filed alphabetically.

At some point it will become unnecessary to write each word on a card. The children, now at stage three, can look at the word, be told what it says, pronounce it once or twice, and then write it from memory. Reading in books usually starts at this time. (Note the similarity here to the "look and say" approach, but with the addition of writing.)

At the fourth and final stage, the children begin to note the resemblance of new words to known words, and it is no longer necessary that they be taught every new word. Phonic sounding of word parts is not allowed in this method, but skill in word analysis gradually develops through the *larger*, similar structural portions.

Children who are having less difficulty in reading may skip the first stage of tracing, but total nonreaders must always start there. Difficult as well as easy words can be taught from the very beginning. Sand trays can be used instead of paper strips for practice.

The major advantages of the kinesthetic method are:

1.   Careful and systematic study of words, with a consistent left-to-right direction of attack, is inherent.

2.   A large amount of repetition and constant checking is provided, and words tend to be retained well.

3.   Errors can be noted and corrected immediately, and because each child keeps a file of the words he or she has learned the child has a good sense of his or her own progress.

4.   The other sensory impressions received from the fingertips and from the writing tend to reinforce the visual and auditory stimuli and are especially important when children are not particularly adequate visual or phonetic learners.

The most often mentioned disadvantages are:

1.   In large groups the amount of time the teacher must spend in making strips, checking, and other tasks may be quite extensive. The teacher must be well organized and preferably should have a smaller group than is usual in the regular classroom.

2.   The method tends to be slow, especially for those who learn readily through visual methods.

3.   The use of books may be put off for some time. This may tend to divorce reading from books in the minds of children and lead to some transfer difficulties.

4.   Young children have a tendency to spill the materials, which must then be picked up and realphabetized.

For more information of this method, see:

Fernald, Grace M. *Remedial Techniques in the Basic School Subjects.* New York: McGraw-Hill, 1943.

## COMBINATIONS OF METHODS

Most teachers today teach reading through a combination of many of these methods, using the basal reader as the vehicle for presentation. There is no question that a combination method, rather than any one of those mentioned separately here, is more likely to help more children learn to read. Since there are differences in learning rate, in kind of thinking, in stimuli that make the greatest impression, and in every other aspect of learning among individuals, it is only reasonable to attempt to reach more of these individuals by including parts of many methods.

Teachers reading this explanation of "pure" methods should try to adapt ideas from those presented for the benefit of their own classes and should *never* attempt to become complete "purists" in method. Utilizing a single method in teaching reading to the exclusion of other methods may have the unfortunate effect of excluding some children from the possibility of learning.

# 3 SPECIAL APPROACHES

In the preceding chapter the word "method" was used very often, primarily because "methods of teaching" has a lengthy pedagogical history. However, many of the methods could more properly be called "approaches" to the teaching of reading, particularly since no single one has guaranteed efficacy and many are utilized in combination (as in the classroom employing basal readers). In addition, such approaches as phonics and oral reading deserve a larger treatment because of their importance and widespread use. This chapter, therefore, discusses two newer organizational arrangements which could utilize *all* the methods discussed previously and gives more information on both phonics and oral reading.

## INDIVIDUALIZED READING

Individualized reading, as an organizational plan for teaching, continues to gain advocates. There are great variations as to how it should be implemented in the classroom, however. It is based on the principles of seeking, self-selection, and pacing, as outlined in the early 1940s by Willard Olson.

In the "pure" approach, each child selects a book he or she wants to read from an extensive classroom library. The teacher schedules individual conferences with each child, ordinarily from five to ten minutes in length. During a portion of this time, the child reads orally to the teacher. Careful records are kept on each individual, and in addition to asking questions about the reading, the teacher may help with skill problems as they show themselves. It is also possible to set up small groups of children for skill-building lessons if several are having the same difficulties.

Most teachers utilize a wide variety of trade books rather than basal readers. Some also incorporate multilevel materials.[1] At the primary-grade level, experience stories may be used heavily, particularly in initial stages.

[1] Two multilevel series of reading materials are *SRA Reading Laboratories* (Chicago: Science Research Associates, 1961); and *Lessons for Self-Instruction* (Monterey, Calif.: CTB/McGraw-Hill, 1963).

(In the beginning stages, total independence in reading is unlikely, and many more group lessons are needed, particularly in phonics and other word-recognition skills.) In general, the approach is better adapted to the inter-mediate rather than the primary grades because of both materials and skills problems. The amount of new vocabulary in *any* new trade book may be overwhelming, and the necessary skills for independence in word attack take time to build. Therefore, some sophistication in reading is needed before complete individualization is possible.

Though careful evaluation has not yet been completed, this method appears to have the following advantages:

—Self-selection of materials keeps interest and motivation at a high level.

—Individual differences in ability are taken into account to a greater extent than by any system of grouping, and individual teaching more nearly reaches particular problems. Children are not compared directly with one another.

—A larger amount of reading seems to result.

—A closer personal relationship between the teacher and child may result from the individual conference sessions.

—Independent work habits, self-confidence, and self-direction tend to be fostered.

The method also has certain limitations:

—The skill-building program is difficult to handle, since every child is reading in a different book, using different words, and meeting different problems. Systematic instruction in these skills may be lacking.

—Record-keeping in a large class can become a major problem.

—Children do not always select reading books on a level at which they can profit. Research suggests that children vary the grade level of their choices continually.

—In cases of difficult problems too much extra time may be devoted to particular individuals who cannot profit from it to a justifiable degree.

—The advantages to working with others in a group at least a part of the time are ignored in a completely individualized approach.

For further discussion of the approach and general techniques, see:

Barbe, Walter. *Educator's Guide to Personalized Reading Instruction.* Engle-wood Cliffs, N.J.: Prentice-Hall, 1966.

Hunt, Lyman C., Jr. "Individualized Reading" and "The Key to the Confer-ence Lies in Questioning," in Frank P. Greene, ed., *Reading: Reasons and Readiness.* Syracuse, N.Y.: Syracuse University Press, 1970.

McCracken, Robert A., and McCracken, Marlene J. *Reading Is Only the Tiger's Tail.* San Rafael, Calif.: Leswing Press, 1972.

Miller, Wilma H. *The First R: Elementary Reading Today.* New York: Holt, Rinehart & Winston, 1972.

Olson, Willard C. "Reading as a Function of Total Growth," in *Reading in Pupil Development*. Supplementary Educational Monographs, No. 51. Chicago: University of Chicago Press, 1940.

Veatch, Jeannette. *Individualizing Your Reading*. New York: G. P. Putnam's Sons, 1959.

————. *Reading in the Elementary School*. New York: Ronald Press, 1966.

## LEARNING STATIONS

As a way to individualize while still keeping the advantages of group work and cutting down somewhat on multiplicity of plans, learning stations are becoming increasingly popular. A learning station consists of a group of children working together at a well-defined curricular task. The location may be a group of desks placed together, a table, a carrel, or a spot on the floor or in the hall. The lessons may parallel classroom instruction, reinforce some aspects of teaching, provide enrichment, or integrate many areas of the curriculum for a science or social studies project. It is a plan to teach not only reading but its many uses.

As much as possible, the lesson plan posted at each station should be self-directing. Supplies which are necessary are located there. The teacher acts as a resource person and gives individual assistance after a general introduction of the task to the group. A number of learning stations are in operation at the same time, and children may, according to plan, circulate as a group during the day or the week.

Possibilities in this form of organization are limited only by the creativity and planning ability of the teacher and tend to increase and improve with each year it is used. However, just as in any form of individualization, it is best done with a qualified aide in the room who understands both the curriculum and the children well.

The advantages seem to be:

—Much individualization is possible without losing the positive effects of small group work and cooperation.

—A great variety of curricular approaches is possible, so motivation is high.

—The teacher has an opportunity to help individuals with their problems connected always with a job which the child is doing, so difficulties tend to be well focused.

But there are also disadvantages:

—The amount of planning is considerable and must include real care in providing for self-directive instructions and tasks which may be shared in the group.

—This is not, perhaps, as adequate an approach to the teaching of reading. Rather, it is using reading. As a consequence, the poor readers in the class may often feel left out and will need a great deal of help to operate in the group.

Many specific suggestions will be found in:

Godfrey, Lorraine Lunt. *Individualize with Learning Station Themes.* Menlo Park, Calif.: Individualized Books, 1974.

————. *Individualizing Through Learning Stations.* Menlo Park, Calif.: Individualized Books, 1972.

## WHAT ABOUT PHONICS?

### *History and Limitations of the Method*

When independence in word attack is mentioned, there are some who feel that the entire process is expressed by the word "phonics." Phonics, however, is not enough. Unknown words are first approached through context clues (the meaning of the surrounding words), and context clues must be used to check back after purely phonetic methods have been applied. Secondly, the pupil who is reading for meaning will look for picture clues, if the book has them. Next he or she will probably look for known word parts or any structural clues. If all else fails, the pupil will take the sound of each learned letter or letter combination and attempt to blend this sound softly with other sounds in order to say the entire word. Then he or she will check this sound against the meaning of the word in the context.

The only time in American school history that a complete sight-word method of reading instruction was advocated was the period from about 1840 to 1890. Another low point for the inclusion of phonics in reading was in the 1930s. At both times this trend stemmed from public and professional reaction to overuse of the phonetic method and the problems that resulted. The consequent "overswing" toward the word method eventually induced an opposite reaction. Present-day teachers' guides and methods courses consistently suggest a combination method that includes the teaching of phonetic analysis with other methods of word recognition in a meaningful setting.

In the 175 years that have elapsed since instruction in phonics was first introduced in America, a great deal has been learned about its use. We, as teachers, should build our reading program on the results of research and experience, and not on some preconceived, self-designated "logical" framework.

There are a few specialists who believe wholeheartedly in the purely phonetic approach. They do not agree, however, on what this approach should be. Rudolph Flesch, in *Why Johnny Can't Read* (New York: Harper & Row, 1955), declares that if his plan is not followed without deviation, success is not likely. In *The Writing Road to Reading*, Romalda and Walter Spalding (New York: Morrow, 1957) give the same caution, but a different method. The same is true for Lewis Terman and Charles Walcutt's *Reading: Chaos and Cure* (New York: McGraw-Hill, 1958). Most of the pure phonics books give lists of words for drill; some give games that can be played to help in the learning of the lists; some insist on the writing of the words, with spelling as the major emphasis. Some teach the names of the letters, others the sounds. Some give several sounds for consonants; others give only one. The vowels differ too. Lorna C. Reed and Donald S. Klopp's *Phonics for Thought* (New York: Comet, 1957) teaches the short vowel sounds first while *The Phonetic Keys to Reading* by Theodore L. Harris and others (Oklahoma City, Okla.: Economy, 1952) teaches the long vowels first. These examples should be sufficient to show that there is little agreement on how or what to teach in phonics even among the so-called phonics experts.

English is not a particularly phonetic language. Well over one hundred sounds are produced by the twenty-six letters of the alphabet; moreover, what is correct in one part of the United States is not necessarily correct in another. One of the biggest problems is the unstressed vowel sound (the schwa), which may be spelled in thirty different ways. The following poem is a good example of our difficulty with phonics in the English language.

> When the English tongue we speak
> Why is *break* not rhymed with *freak*?
> Will you tell me why it's true
> We say *sew*, but likewise *few*;
> And the maker of a verse
> Cannot cap his *horse* with *worse*?
> *Beard* sounds not the same as *heard*;
> *Cord* is different from *word*;
> Cow is *cow* but low is *low*;
> *Shoe* is never rhymed with *foe*.
> Think of *hose* and *dose* and *lose*;
> And think of *goose* and yet of *choose*.
> Think of *comb* and *tomb* and *bomb*;
> *Doll* and *roll* and *home* and *some*;
> And since *pay* is rhymed with *say*,
> Why not *paid* with *said*, I pray?
> We have *blood* and *food* and *good*;
> *Mould* is not pronounced like *could*.
> Wherefore *done* but *gone* and *lone*?
> Is there any reason known?
> And, in short, it seems to me
> Sounds and letters disagree.

English has evolved from many other languages. It follows no strict pattern of pronunciation. Consequently, no single method of word attack can be depended upon. As the student meets more involved words of several syllables, this becomes even more apparent. That is why many methods of attacking new words must be taught to pupils in the modern reading program, not simply phonics alone. On the other hand, phonics cannot be skipped. It is one of the important methods of word attack.

### Teaching Phonics

Researchers have concluded that in teaching phonics, certain practices produce better results than others. Beginning readers should first master some sight vocabulary with consistent phonetic elements before starting to learn phonics formally. Phonics should be introduced using an inductive approach, not by stating a rule. Children should discover the principle by observing common characteristics in the words used, both visually and auditorially; they can then apply the discovered principle to other words to see how it works. Consonant rather than vowel sounds are the best starting point because they are easier to hear and to learn. Following the order of presentation in the teacher's manual accompanying the basal series used is also generally wise. The phonics are thus directly tied to the reading vocabulary, and the skills are learned in developmental sequence. Such instruction in phonics should continue throughout the elementary school because children need reteaching and review to fully absorb phonic lessons.

In addition to these research findings on the effective teaching of phonics it would be helpful to keep in mind a few practical don'ts:

1. Never call letters by their sounds; use their alphabetical names instead. It is the word that determines the particular sound of most English letters.

2. Do not interject phonics into the middle of the oral reading part of the lesson. Tell the word quickly and show how to analyze it later.

3. Never drill for the sake of drilling. Phonics and other recognition skills should be taught as a part of the directed reading activity. The words used must come from the reading or meaning will be lost.

4. In general, avoid phonetic rules. Students do not bother to recall the rule; they apply the generalization.

5. Do not have the group respond in chorus because that masks what the individual child is saying.

6. Avoid distortions of words. A word should never be broken into independent sounds but should be spoken as a unit.

When phonics is used as the basic method in teaching reading, research has shown both positive and negative results. On the positive side, the method definitely improves children's oral skill and pronunciation and sometimes improves their word-recognition skill. But negatively, it tends to produce slower readers because it encourages the piecemeal recognition of words. Moreover, the method produces no superiority in reading comprehension.

It is essential that any teacher of reading know both sides of the teaching of reading through phonics. Because of the fact that phonics is an apparently logical system of teaching reading, it tends to be overly attractive to parents, particularly when their child is having difficulty in learning. It is not, however, always as motivating to those same children.

The references following are suggested as an approach to the theory and the limitations. Materials which might be utilized in particular cases will be suggested in the section on word attack in the next chapter.

Fry, Edward. *Reading Instruction for Classroom and Clinic.* New York: McGraw-Hill, 1972.

Gray, William S. *On Their Own in Reading.* 2nd ed. Chicago: Scott, Foresman, 1960.

Heilman, Arthur W. *Phonics in Proper Perspective.* Columbus, Ohio: Charles E. Merrill, 1968.

Spache, George D., and Spache, Evelyn B. *Reading in the Elementary School.* Boston: Allyn & Bacon, 1969.

Spache, George D. *Toward Better Reading.* Champaign, Ill.: Garrard, 1963.

## ORAL READING

### Usefulness of the Method

Fifty years ago all reading instruction in the schools was oral reading instruction. In the 1920s a definite shift toward silent reading instruction occurred. The basic reasons advanced for this shift were that (1) most reading done outside the school is silent reading, and the schools should prepare children for the situation they will meet as adults; and (2) silent reading emphasizes meaning rather than sound, and the major emphasis in reading should be meaning.

Most children and adults, however, meet occasional situations in which it is important that they be able to read well orally. Some kinds of reading material such as poetry are not as satisfying when read silently. Oral reading gives the teacher a good basis for appraisal of progress in pronunciation, expression, comprehension, word recognition, and word attack. It also permits diagnosis of individual problems. In the beginning stages oral reading helps the child associate the printed word with the spoken word. For these reasons, oral reading is still with us today, and should be.

In general, oral reading instruction should:

Develop the child's eye-voice span

Provide a genuine audience situation

Teach enunciation, phrasing and emphasis

Help children share enjoyment with others

Enable children who have difficulty with the printed form to understand ideas by listening to them as they are read aloud

## Teaching Oral Reading

Most children enjoy reading to each other and should be given the opportunity to do so in a meaningful way. The poorest readers often need the greatest number of opportunities. Successful experiences in oral reading may help to combat shyness and to boost self-confidence, needs shared by good and poor readers alike. However, care must be taken to provide opportunities that will lead to success, not failure. As with the teaching of phonics, certain practices have been found better than others in promoting success.

A most important practice is to provide students with good examples they can imitate. The teacher is primarily responsible for setting this good example and should do so often. But parents may also be called on if they have been found to be exceptionally good oral readers and can volunteer the time. Records or tapes may be used as well.

When the children seem receptive to trying it themselves, they should be given some preparation time with the materials to be read orally, so it is a good idea to give them a chance to read it silently first. Above the first-grade level of reading, listeners *should never follow in their books.* Allowing listeners to follow actually defeats the purposes of oral reading. It encourages poor reading habits in the followers because eye movements are not smooth and students often lose their place. By making the listeners a group of checkers rather than an audience, it also creates an embarrassing situation for the oral reader and makes him or her nervous. Furthermore, instead of providing an excellent opportunity for training in listening skills, an area that we have been inclined to neglect, it destroys the listening situation. The mechanics of a good oral reading situation are easier than they seem: merely pass the book to the next reader, indicating the place as it is passed. Then check the comprehension of the *listeners*, not the reader.

One final practice that makes for success in oral reading is to provide a wide range of materials for such reading. Materials that derive from activities in the classroom are especially good because they have a definite purpose. Thus, reading announcements, construction plans, or directions, giving talks, telling jokes and riddles for fun (edited!), and sharing information, plans, creative stories, or poems with others are all acceptable oral reading situations. Practice objectives might also be achieved through choral reading and reading into a tape recorder for more careful evaluation.

The teacher who is evaluating a child in oral reading should be conscious of:

Ability in word recognition, pronunciation, and enunciation

Indications that meaning is known and that the child is attempting to communicate this meaning (by emphasis or inflection)

Variety and appropriateness of tone, pitch, force, and speed

Whether the pupil appears at ease and whether he is conscious of and responsive to the reactions of his audience

Whether the reader exhibits interest and enthusiasm, giving his own interpretation of the selection

Whether posture is erect and dignified without being stiff and over-formal

For more information on teaching oral reading, see:

Harris, Albert J. *How to Increase Reading Ability*. 5th ed. New York: David McKay, 1970.

Tinker, Miles A., and McCullough, Constance M. *Teaching Elementary Reading*. 3rd ed. New York: Appleton-Century-Crofts, 1968.

# *4* THE IMPROVEMENT OF SPECIFIC READING SKILLS

## WORD RECOGNITION

Severely retarded readers show their greatest deficiency in word recognition. Success in reading usually comes when words are recognized quickly and accurately so that the reader is freed to concentrate on meaning. Pupils who have much difficulty recognizing words interrupt their train of thought so frequently to recall the word itself that they end up with little idea of the content covered. They have to slow down or even stop completely to use word-attack skills or to use the context to identify a word. In the process of determining what the words are, they simply lose the thought behind the words.

Whenever "new" words occur in reading, some word-recognition problems arise. This happens at all levels of reading because most children do not learn to recognize a new word at the first meeting but must meet the word in varying contexts before it is firmly established as a sight word. It is important for the teacher to remember, however, that until almost all words in the material are well known as sight words, the comprehension of the reader is likely to suffer. Rapid word recognition is an important objective in the teaching of reading.

Children may be helped to learn sight words in various ways. The story in the basal reader helps the teacher introduce new words. Saying the word (in context) and simultaneously writing it on the chalkboard or using cards and a pocket chart will give a spoken and visual form to the new words. Children may be asked to "frame" words with their hands, to make up sentences using new words in the pocket chart, to read chart stories or chalkboard stories containing the new words, to match words to pictures, to select word cards, or to use a picture dictionary or their workbook. In these ways, attention is called to special characteristics of new words. The spoken word is correlated with the printed word, and children are given much practice in the use of the word. Workbooks usually provide systematic visual study of these same words, make the meanings clear, and provide a transition to silent reading.

34

There are, then, many different approaches to word recognition. They may be summarized as:

Picture clues, where the picture is presented with the new word or accompanies it in the text

Visual repetition, where the new form is presented with the known spoken form or with meaning clues

Shape or configurational clues such as the tail at the end of the word "monkey"

Familiar parts, especially in compound words such as *butterfly*

Context clues, where the meaning of the new word becomes more obvious because of the rest of the sentence in which it is included

Dictionary aids to pronunciation and meaning

Phonetic and structural analysis (presented separately in the following section)

Obviously, the skillful reader does not have to rely exclusively on any single method in order to recognize words. Further, all of the above approaches are interrelated. It is very difficult, for example, to apply phonetic and structural analysis without attention to context clues.

Some words are common in all writing at all levels, so that without a knowledge of these basic words, students can read hardly anything. The best-known list of common words is that given by E. W. Dolch,[1] containing 220 words, or approximately one-half of the words commonly found in all written material, exclusive of nouns. Other such word lists are available from many sources. Basic word lists that are carefully researched have been used in selecting the vocabulary for basal readers. Therefore, for a practical source teachers may use the word lists in the back of their basal readers, disregarding only names and content-oriented nouns.

Besides the general problem of gaining a sufficient sight vocabulary, beginning readers often have one or a number of the following specific word-recognition problems:

Reversals and inversions of words and letters (e.g., *was* for *saw*, or *no* for *on*)

Substitutions of words that resemble others in meaning or form (e.g., *house* for *home*)

Omissions, where words or parts of words are skipped, changing the meaning of the sentence

Insertions, when words that are not present on the page are added by the reader

Repetitions, where the reader goes back over words or parts of sentences either orally or silently

Hesitations, where the reader eventually recognizes the word, but only

[1] *A Manual for Remedial Reading* (Champaign, Ill.: Garrard, 1945).

after pausing; this is word-by-word reading if the reader pauses for every word

Complete stops, where the reader is unable to attempt the word and must look to the teacher for help

### Ways to Improve Word-Recognition Skills

Table 4.1 lists some specific methods and materials that may be used to improve word-recognition skills. There are also some general principles that teachers can follow. Most important is to use a variety of approaches so that students become aware of a number of clues to word recognition. Preparation is also important. Teachers should not fall back on isolated drills but instead find meaningful materials so that word recognition becomes not merely word calling but meaning recognition. In using such material, teachers should ascertain whether students know or have the background necessary to derive the meaning of the words they are trying to identify.

The key habit that students must acquire is the ability to inspect words rapidly, thoroughly, and systematically from left to right. Therefore, visual training—giving students the ability to spot similarities and differences among words and to locate a known element in an unknown word—takes priority over training in sounding words out. The specific techniques suggested in Table 4.1 should help in this visual training.

Many of the methods outlined in Table 4.1 are concerned with oral reading. Oral reading affords the opportunity for diagnosis by the teacher since it is the most obvious demonstration of the learner's problems. It is interesting to observe that, in spite of this, many poor readers will ask to read orally. Very probably, the poor reader realizes that this is the best way for him or her to draw attention to a specific problem.

Note, too, that word-attack skills must be related to the word-recognition skills since it is always a question of finding out what the unknown word is by one means or another. It is possible for many pupils to gain a very large sight vocabulary by merely having someone "tell" the word, although this means, in turn, that they cannot progress very far independently. Thus the next section, which discusses word attack, is very highly related to this section on word recognition.

For further information on word recognition, see:

Dallmann, Martha, et al. *The Teaching of Reading.* 4th ed. New York: Holt, Rinehart & Winston, 1974. Chapters 5A and 5B.

Hafner, Lawrence E., and Jolly, Hayden B. *Patterns of Teaching Reading in the Elementary School.* New York: Macmillan, 1972. Chapter 5.

Karlin, Robert. *Teaching Elementary Reading; Principles and Strategies.* 2nd ed. New York: Harcourt Brace Jovanovich, 1975. Chapters 5 and 6.

Kennedy, Eddie C. *Classroom Approaches to Remedial Reading.* Itasca, Ill.: F. E. Peacock, 1971. Chapter 11.

## TABLE 4.1 METHODS FOR TEACHING WORD RECOGNITION

| Objective | Procedures | References and Materials |
|---|---|---|
| To overcome reversals or inversions of words or letters within words; to help those who have difficulty with left-to-right movement | Have children trace the form of the word, saying the word (in syllables if possible) as they trace; then have them attempt to write the word without looking and check back. If they make a mistake, have them retrace the word. | Adapted from Fernald, Grace. *Remedial Techniques in the Basic School Subjects.* New York: McGraw-Hill, 1943. |
| | Let the children make their own dictionaries of new words, emphasizing alphabetical arrangement. | A spiral notebook or a file box of cards |
| | Give completion sentences in which the proper word must be written, as, "The boy (was, saw) _____ the car." | Dittoed work sheets |
| | Use flash cards for words that have been confused. A student having particular difficulty can say the words to another who knows them. | Flash cards of pre-primer and primer words available from publishers of basal readers |
| | Have students write the words in manuscript or type them. If available, a typewriter is best. | Old typewriter |
| | Call attention to the letter clue at the beginning. Perhaps use green color for beginning letter and red for the ending letter (stop and go colors), or underline first and last letter in the colors. | See Dallmann, Martha, et al. *The Teaching of Reading.* 4th ed. New York: Holt, Rinehart & Winston, 1974, Chapter 5. |

| Objective | Procedures | References and Materials |
|---|---|---|
| To increase sight vocabulary | On the chalkboard in columns, place several words that may be confused with one another. Point to a word and have children identify it; or name a word and have a pupil point to the word named. | |
| | Present new words in sentences on the board or on charts. Emphasize experience of peers. Use the word orally *before* a pupil attempts to read it. | Teachers' guides for basal readers |
| | Ditto a sheet with groups of three or four words of similar configuration. Have children circle the word read to them. | |
| | Play "Wordo," an adaptation of Bingo, or other sight-word games. | Commercial form available from Garrard; Champaign, Ill. |
| | Use the dictionary to determine meaning differences. | *Thorndike - Barnhart Beginning Dictionary.* New York: Doubleday, 1972. |
| | Have children read into the tape recorder and listen as they play it back to discover errors. | Tape recorder |
| | Use phrase flash cards or a phrase tachistoscope. | For games, etc. see Spache, Evelyn B. *Reading Activities for Child Involvement.* Boston: Allyn & Bacon, 1972. |

| Objective | Procedures | References and Materials |
|---|---|---|
| To overcome the omission of words or letters | Have a child reread the passage where the word is omitted. If omitted the second time, ask for it specifically. During oral reading, supply the word, make a note of it, and return to word attack after the oral reading. | |
| | Check for speech and visual problems if letter sounds are omitted. | |
| | If carelessness seems to be the reason for the omissions:<br>1. Have the student read into the tape recorder and then listen to the playback, following in the book.<br>2. Ask detailed questions concerned with the omission. Read back to prove. (All others should have their books closed during oral reading beyond first-reader level.) | Tape recorder and basal or supplementary readers |
| | 3. Attempt to find more interesting material. | Instructional Materials Center. |
| | Provide a "Help Yourself" box. After completing regular work, the children draw a slip of paper and follow the directions. For example: "Here is a picture of a sad old hen. Make up a story to tell what makes the hen so sad." | Shoe box or something similar |

| _Objective_ | _Procedures_ | _References and Materials_ |
|---|---|---|
| To overcome hesitations and repetitions | Be sure that silent reading precedes oral reading. | |
| | Do choral reading, emphasizing phrasing. | Possien, Wilma M. _They All Need to Talk._ New York: Appleton-Century-Crofts, 1969. |
| | Dramatize stories (especially the conversational portions), or use radio plays. | _Plays._ Plays, Inc.; Boston, Mass. (a periodical) |
| | Promote as much self-confidence as possible since hesitation in reading is usually an indication of insecurity. Strive for informality and praise. | |
| | Discourage finger pointing, lip movement, and vocalization. | |
| To train in the use of configuration clues | Direct attention to likenesses and differences in words by using the board. Ask pupils to look for: | |

Direct attention to likenesses and differences in words by using the board. Ask pupils to look for:

1. Similarities in words (marking the board or framing words with the hands) like
   _eat_     cr_eam_
2. Differences in words like
   ea_t_     _cream_
3. Differences in length like
   boy     birthday
4. Differences in shapes of words like
   happy     big

| Objective | Procedures | References and Materials |
|-----------|------------|--------------------------|
| | 5. Differences in meaning like<br>cool    cold | |
| To build skill in the use of context clues | Give exercises that require the anticipation of meaning. Use examples such as "George _____ home after school." Pupils suggest words that could fit, such as *walked* or *hurried*. If a specific word is wanted, give clues: "It begins with *r*." | For lists of commercial materials and activities and games for the classroom, see: Schubert, Delwyn, and Torgerson, Theodore. *Improving the Reading Program*. 3rd ed. Dubuque, Iowa: William C. Brown, 1972. Chapter 9. |
| | Discuss appropriate techniques of using context:<br>1. Read the *entire* sentence.<br>2. Look at the beginning and ending sounds of the word, and think of a suitable word that begins and ends the same way.<br>3. Read the entire paragraph if necessary. | Spache, Evelyn B. *Reading Activities for Child Involvement*. Boston: Allyn & Bacon, 1972. Chapter 8. |
| | Use the dictionary and construct exercises such as the one below to show multiple meanings:<br>DIRECTIONS: *Write the letter of the definition in the space next to the sentence.*<br>1. ——He rattled on with the story.<br>2. ——He was rattled by the tales told to him. | |

| Objective | Procedures | References and Materials |
|-----------|------------|--------------------------|
| | 3. ——The dishes rattled in the sink. | |
| | 4. ——The baby shook his rattle. | |
| |    a.  rapid succession of noises | |
| |    b.  confused | |
| |    c.  chattered | |
| |    d.  a toy | |

## WORD ATTACK

Phonetic analysis, structural analysis, and the use of the dictionary are usually included in the word-attack skills. Chapter 3 presented a discussion of phonetic analysis, including conclusions of research and some generalizations which have grown out of practice. This section will include some specific methods and materials in phonics, plus specific methods and materials in structural analysis and the use of the dictionary.

The sequence of activities in a basal series usually proceeds in a given order, according to reading levels. The reading levels are not necessarily the grade placement levels, since reading level and grade placement are often different. The list below summarizes the order. But keep in mind that in several recent series, these skills are placed about one book lower in the sequence, where the emphasis is on phonics and/or structural linguistics.

### Pre-Primer
Distinguishing ending rhymes
Hearing initial consonant sounds

### Primer
Recognizing a few compound words from previously known words
(some + thing = something)
Hearing and seeing likenesses in initial consonants
Making initial consonant substitutions (*n*ame, *s*ame)

### Book One
Hearing and seeing final consonants
Using both initial and final consonant substitutions
Recognizing the different forms of words made by adding *s, 's, ed, ing*

Recognizing the digraphs *wh*, *ch*, *sh*, *th*

Recognizing the consonant blends *br*, *fl*, *st*, *tr*, and others

Finding "little words in big words" (with caution here, because of changes like *at* in h*at* and g*ate*, *up* in c*up* and p*up*il)

## Book Two

Recognizing the long and short vowels, using rules for determining sounds of vowels

Recognizing the different sounds of some consonants, as *c* in *cat* and *city*

Learning certain spelling rules:

to double the final consonant before the ending (swi*m*, swi*mm*ing)

to change the final *y* to *i* (hurr*y*, hurr*i*ed)

to drop the final *e* (ri*d*e, riding)

Recognizing forms of words that are already known in the sight vocabulary but which have the endings *es*, *er*, *est*, *ly*, *n*, *en* added to root words

## Book Three

Learning variant vowel sounds:

vowel affected by *r*

*a* followed by *l* or *w*

the schwa (*a* in *a*bout, *e* in tak*e*n, *i* in penc*i*l, *o* in lem*o*n, *u* in circ*u*s)

Recognizing more digraphs, such as *ea*, *ai*, *oa* and diphthongs, such as *oi*, *oy*, *ou*, *ow*

Identifying and learning the meanings of prefixes (*un-*, *im-*, *dis-*) and suffixes (*-ful*, *-ish*, *-ness*, *-less*)

Working with some root words

Beginning to apply the principles of syllabication, applying vowel principles to syllables

Beginning work with accent and its effect on vowel sounds

## Book Four & Higher

Developing dictionary skills (location, selection, pronunciation)

Studying synonyms, antonyms, homonyms, multiple meanings

Reviewing all previous phonetic and structural learnings

Giving further practice in combining all methods on new words

Noting structural analysis of more difficult words; primary and secondary accent

Using principles of syllabication

Though this is a careful sequence of phonetic analysis, structural activities, and dictionary usage, no teacher should assume that children will be able to apply all these skills. If a skill has been presented to children before they are ready, they will act as though they have never heard of it. Furthermore, some teachers still skip portions of the teacher's guide or have such large classes that they cannot do a careful job on all such activities. As a result a few children will not have had experience with a particular skill. Reteaching and review are, therefore, especially important in this area of reading.

Separate and distinct phonics books or separate periods for instruction in phonics are employed by some school districts. This may be necessary in some situations, but in general, special instruction in phonics is more important in remedial work with older pupils than as a common practice with all pupils from the beginning of the reading program. In case a district would like to investigate such materials, however, the following are representative:

Cordts, Anna. *Functional Phonetics and Readiness for Power in Reading.* Chicago: Beckley-Cardy.

Durrell, Donald D., and Sullivan, Helen B. *Building Word Power and Ready to Read Workbook.* New York: Harcourt Brace Jovanovich, 1960.

Hay, Julie, and Wingo, Charles. *Reading with Phonics.* Philadelphia: J. B. Lippincott, 1967.

Herr, Selma. *Phonics.* Los Angeles: Educational Research Associates, 1962.

Johnson, Eleanor. *Phonics SkillTexts.* Columbus, Ohio: Charles E. Merrill.

Meighen, Mary, Pratt, Marjorie, and Halvorsen, Mabel. *Phonics We Use.* Chicago: Lyons & Carnahan, 1962.

Sloop, Cornelia B. *The Phonetic Keys to Reading.* Oklahoma City, Oklahoma: Economy, 1952.

Stone, Clarence. *Eye and Ear Fun.* St. Louis: Webster, 1946.

Stratemeyer, Clara, and Smith, Henry Lee, Jr. *The Linguistic-Science Readers.* New York: Harper & Row, 1963.

Thompson, Lola M. *Happy Times with Sounds.* Boston: Allyn & Bacon, 1960.

Most of the above consist of a series of workbooks to use at reading levels from one through three while some also have materials to use at the fourth level and above.

There are also a number of records and filmstrips useful in this connection:

"Basic Primary Phonics." Chicago: Society for Visual Education.

"Filmstrips for Practice in Phonetic Skills." Chicago: Scott, Foresman.

Kottmeyer, William, and Ware, Kay. "New Spelling Goals Filmstrips." St. Louis: Webster.

"Let's Listen" (album). Boston: Ginn.

"Phonics" (four filmstrips). Chicago: Scott, Foresman.

"Sounds Around Us." Chicago: Scott, Foresman.

"Textfilms in Reading." New York: Harper & Row.

### How to Teach Word-Attack Skills

Table 4.2 shows a listing of specific methods designed for teaching the word-attack skills. These should be correlated directly with the words in the reading materials being used currently. Pupils should have opportunities to apply each skill as it is introduced, and practice should continue periodically.

## TABLE 4.2 METHODS FOR TEACHING WORD ATTACK

| Objective | Procedures | References and Materials |
|---|---|---|
| To develop auditory perception | Before beginning a lesson in phonic analysis, make sure that the pupils can first hear the sound of the element being taught. For example, have the pupils give orally another word beginning (or ending) with the same sound as the one given. Then write both words on the board. | Russell, David, and Karp, Eta. *Reading Aids Through the Grades.* New York: Teachers College Press, Columbia University, 1951. |
| | Illustrate the sounds whenever possible. For example, the explosive *p* is shown by placing a piece of thin paper in front of the lips and saying words beginning with *p*. Pupils may try this out for themselves and make lists of the words. | Gray, William S. *On Their Own in Reading.* 2nd ed. Chicago: Scott, Foresman, 1960. |
| | Have children watch your lips while saying "fire," "fast," "farm," "fine." They may observe their own lips in a mirror. They then note both their own and your lips while "house," "hurt," "heavy," and "had" are pro- | Heilman, Arthur. *Phonics in Proper Perspective.* Columbus, Ohio: Charles E. Merrill, 1968.<br><br>Spache, George D., and Spache, Evelyn B. *Reading in the Elemen-* |

| Objective | Procedures | References and Materials |
|---|---|---|
| | nounced. Children should then indicate which of these words begin with *f* and which begin with *h*. | *tary School.* Boston: Allyn & Bacon, 1969. |
| To relate auditory and visual perception | To teach initial consonant: (1) write several known words beginning with the same letter and sound; (2) have the words read; (3) ask for the part that looks alike in all the words; (4) set off the beginning letter but do not isolate it; (5) pronounce the words so that children hear the sound; (6) have a child pronounce the words; (7) have the children try to think of other words; and (8) write illustrative words on the board and compare (go, get, gave, good).<br><br>Also, while the children close their eyes and listen, say several words, only some of which begin with the new consonant. Children clap once when they hear a word that begins with the new consonant sound. | Write to the publisher of the materials you are using for free materials concerned with phonic and structural analysis. For variety, try: *Linguistic Block Series.* Chicago: Scott, Foresman.<br><br>*Speech-to-Print Phonics.* New York: Harcourt Brace Jovanovich.<br><br>"Webster Word Analysis Charts." Manchester, Mo.: Webster 'McGraw-Hill.<br><br>"Webster Word Wheels." Manchester, Mo.: Webster/McGraw-Hill.<br><br>"Vowel Lotto." Champaign, Ill.: Garrard. |
| | To teach short vowel sounds: (1) write a list of one-syllable words with the same vowel sound; (2) have the pupils pronounce each word and underline the short vowel; (3) use other words; (4) | For phonics games, write for "What the Letters Say," "Consonant Lotto," "Vowel Lotto," and "Take." Champaign, Ill.: Garrard. |

| Objective | Procedures | References and Materials |
|---|---|---|
| | help pupils verbalize the rule: if there is one vowel in a word and it is not at the end, the vowel is *usually* short. | |
| | For teaching final *e*, make exercises requiring choice of the correct word:<br>1. Mother (mad, made) me a cake.<br>2. The toy will cost a (dim, dime).<br>3. We (plan, plane) to make a trip. | |
| | For vowel digraphs, have children underline the vowel sound *heard* in words such as sleet, reach, sneak, grain, float, or have them circle the sounded vowel and cross out the silent vowel. | |
| To develop ability in structural analysis | Give pupils exercises in:<br>1. Making new words by adding letters to the ends of other words:<br>  a. What is a chair that rocks? (rocker)<br>  b. What do we call someone who sends something? (sender)<br>2. Finding the number of syllables in each word:<br>  a. little _____<br>  b. page _____<br>  c. understand _____<br>  d. thicket _____ | Useful lists of words such as compound words with endings are to be found in:<br><br>Kottmeyer, William. *Teacher's Guide for Remedial Reading*. Manchester, Mo.: Webster, 1959.<br><br>Heilman, Arthur. *Phonics in Proper Perspective*. Columbus, Ohio: Charles E. Merrill, 1968. |

| *Objective* | *Procedures* | *References and Materials* |
|---|---|---|
| | On the board, have pupils mark the syllables; have them tell why they put the marks where they did. | |
| | Have pupils practice listing as many variations of base words as they can think of: play, plays, played, playing, playmate, player, etc. | Tinker, Miles A., and McCullough, Constance, M. *Teaching Elementary Reading.* 3rd ed. New York: Appleton-Century-Crofts, 1968. |
| | Give children an exercise where they combine a word from one list with one from the other:<br>after   way _____<br>door   noon _____<br>under   ground _____ | |
| | Have children read pairs of sentences, discussing differences in meaning and pronunciation:<br>1.  She wiped a *tear* from her eye.<br>   He had a long *tear* in his shirt.<br>2.  Father *wound* the clock.<br>   The arrow did not *wound* the deer. | |
| To build skill in the use of the dictionary | On a field trip to the library, give children practice in finding books. Explain the functions and use of the unabridged dictionary. | *Thorndike - Barnhart Beginning Dictionary.* New York: Doubleday, 1972. (Has many exercises to teach dictionary usage) |
| | Make exercises to teach the use of guide words. For example, write on the | Fry, Edward, et al. *Lessons for Self Instruction: Use of Ref-* |

| Objective | Procedures | References and Materials |
|---|---|---|
| | board pairs of guide words; then read a list of words aloud and have pupils choose the pair of guide words that indicates the page on which each word will be found. | *erences.* Monterey, Calif.: CTB/McGraw-Hill, 1963. |

Have children arrange scrambled lists of words in alphabetical order to the third letter.

Help pupils become acquainted with all parts of the dictionary—the foreign words, the rhyming section, etc.

Give students dictionary exercises in which they:
1. Look for another word beginning the same way as words given (to the third or fourth letter).
2. Write lists of words (beginning with the same letter) in alphabetical order.
3. Underline two words which mean nearly the same in a line of words.
4. Locate and list, within a set time limit, as many words as they can containing a particular sound element.
5. Fill in words that would fit between given words in a list.

For theoretical discussions and practical ideas for teaching, see:

Chall, Jeanne. *Learning to Read: The Great Debate.* New York: McGraw-Hill, 1967.

Guszak, Frank J. *Diagnostic Reading Instruction in the Elementary School.* New York: Harper & Row, 1972. Chapter 4.

Harris, Albert J. *Readings on Reading Instruction.* New York: David McKay, 1972. Chapter 8.

Heilman, Arthur. *Principles and Practices of Teaching Reading.* 2nd ed. Columbus, Ohio: Charles E. Merrill, 1967. Chapters 8 and 9.

May, Frank B. *To Help Children Read.* Columbus, Ohio: Charles E. Merrill, 1973. Module 2.

Miller, Wilma H. *The First R: Elementary Reading Today.* New York: Holt, Rinehart & Winston, 1972. Chapters 8 and 10.

## COMPREHENSION

Books have been written about the development of creative and critical reading skills, one aspect of deeper comprehension. Often, however, more basic comprehension is necessary before real appreciation and deeper comprehension is possible. This section attempts to describe activities which might be used in the development of basic comprehension.

It should be remembered that the poorer reader with average or better capacity (the retarded reader) will ordinarily comprehend at a level above his or her word-recognition level. He or she will have sufficient ability to partially "outguess" the simpler materials. Without word-recognition and word-attack skills, however, the child's comprehension will be limited, so teaching these skills must precede work on comprehension. On the other hand, many teachers fail to ask questions that call for a variety of comprehension skills. Questions about clearly stated details taken directly from the passage are the easiest ones to phrase and are likely to be asked most often, but full comprehension demands more. Finding the main idea, whether it is stated or inferred, drawing inferences from the story about the story itself, knowing the characters or the plot, and understanding the sequence of ideas in the passage are probably all more important than remembering details.

Table 4.3 lists activities to improve comprehension. The type of comprehension required by the question or involved in the activity is stated in parentheses immediately following the procedure so that teachers may become more conscious of the specific objective. Again, in this presentation, it is not possible to give a complete list of techniques, but the references given should be of help in supplementing those suggested here.

## TABLE 4.3 METHODS FOR IMPROVING COMPREHENSION

| Procedures and Purposes | References and Materials |
|---|---|
| Have children indicate where in a poem or story they first knew it was sad, joyful, humorous, mysterious, etc. (Finding mood expressed by author) | Dallmann, Martha, et al. *The Teaching of Reading.* 4th ed. New York: Holt, Rinehart & Winston, 1974. Chapters 6A and 6B. |
| Give oral or dittoed questions such as the following:<br>1. A bird is fast but a snail is _____.<br>2. The clouds are above, but the ground is _____.<br>3. A horse runs on legs, but a car runs on _____.<br>(Inference) | Duffy, Gerald, and Sherman, George. *How to Teach Reading Systematically.* New York: Harper & Row, 1972. Component No. Six. |
| Prepare a three- or four-sentence story that indicates a sequence of events. Cut it apart by sentences. Pupils are to rearrange the sentences in proper sequence. (Sequence and organization) | King, M. L. ed. *Critical Reading.* Philadelphia: J. B. Lippincott, 1967. |
| From a story pupils have just read, list words and phrases that describe emotional reactions of the characters. Ask pupils to tell which story character experienced each emotional reaction and why. Encourage pupils to refer to specific passages in the story to support their viewpoints. (Inference, tone, and mood) | McCracken, Robert, and McCracken, Marlene. *Reading Is Only the Tiger's Tail.* San Rafael, Calif.: Leswing Press, 1972. Chapter 5. |
| Anticipate vocabulary needs of daily lessons. Present these words in varying contexts, discuss them, and make them as concrete as possible. (Word meaning) | Otto, Wayne, et al. *Focused Reading Instruction.* Reading, Mass.: Addison-Wesley, 1974. Chapter 9. |
| Have children make up new titles for the story. (Main idea) | Russell, David H. *Children Learn to Read.* Rev. ed. Boston: Ginn, 1961, pp. 454–88. |
| During the discussion of the story, ask "why" questions—why various story characters thought, behaved, and reacted as they did. See whether pupils can find passages in the story to support their answers. (Relationships) | Wilson, Robert M., and Hall, Maryanne. *Reading and the Elementary School Child.* New York: Van Nostrand |

| *Procedures and Purposes* | *References and Materials* |
| --- | --- |
| Recall an incident in the story and ask pupils to tell what happened just before and just after the incident. This can also be done by using a picture or the comment of one of the characters. (Sequence of events). | Reinhold, 1972. Chapter 8.<br><br>Zintz, Miles V. *The Reading Process.* Dubuque, Iowa: William C. Brown, 1970. Chapters 8 and 9. |
| Conduct oral discussion periods, encouraging differences of opinion when supported by facts found in the reading. (Main idea) | |
| Skim through a part of the story with children, pointing out pronouns. Have each sentence read and let children tell the person, place, or thing to which each pronoun refers. (Referents) | |
| Have pupils look through a story or article and decide where it can be divided into parts, discussing each part. Have them suggest subtitles that point up the main action of each part. (Organization) | |
| Use workbook materials designed to improve comprehension. | For workbooks to supplement basal readers, see: |
| After a story is read, encourage pupils to imagine what might have happened next. (Inference) | Guiler, W. S., and Coleman, J. H. *Reading for Meaning.* Philadelphia: J. B. Lippincott. |
| Skim a story with children, reviewing the main action in each part. Help children formulate a summary sentence for each part and write the sentences on the board. Have children reread the sentences; then erase them and have pupils tell the story from memory. (Main idea and sequence) | McCall, W. A., and Crabbs, L. M. *Standard Test Lessons in Reading.* New York: Columbia University Press. |
| Have pupils bring recipes, instructions for assembling model planes, directions for mixing starch, | *Reader's Digest Reading Skill Builders.* |

| Procedures and Purposes | References and Materials |
| --- | --- |
| etc. Discuss the need for accuracy in interpreting directions. (Following directions) | Pleasantville, N.Y.: Reader's Digest Educational Division. |
| Have children find phrases showing interesting ways of expressing common ideas. (Figurative language) | Smith, N. *Be a Better Reader*. Englewood Cliffs, N.J.: Prentice-Hall, 1968. |
| Have children read the directions for a new game to play during recess and present the rules to the rest of the class. (Following directions) | |
| Have pupils match headlines to newspaper articles. (Main idea) | |
| Have pupils list or discuss the techniques an author uses to make them like or dislike a character. (Intent of author) | |
| Use multilevel materials for general comprehension (*Reading Laboratory*), special aspects of comprehension (*Reading for Understanding*), or specific skills (*Organizing and Reporting Skills Kit*). | Parker, Donald. *Reading Laboratories*. Thurstone, Thelma. *Reading for Understanding*. Naslund, Robert. *Organizing and Reporting Skills*. Chicago: Science Research Associates. |
| Use branching programmed materials available for the third through ninth grades in *Lessons for Self-Instruction*. | Fry, et al. *Lessons for Self-Instruction: Reading Interpretation*. Monterey, Calif.: CTB/ McGraw-Hill. |

## RATE OF READING

Today, both in school and on the job, we are expected to read and comprehend a much greater volume of material than ever before. Elementary school pupils who are progressing normally, for example, have approximately five times as much required reading in their classes as did elementary children only sixty years ago.

The poor reader is often a slow reader. If he or she is reading below sixth-grade level, this is to be expected. Difficulties in word recognition, in comprehension, in word meaning, and in word attack obviously slow down reading. A direct attack on slow reading is not ordinarily a good idea if basic skills are still being developed. Work should be done, instead, on the improvement of sight vocabulary, on phrasing in oral reading, and on wider practice—always with an emphasis on comprehension. In addition, habits such as finger pointing, excessive head movements, or vocalization should be eliminated.

The direct teaching of speeded reading is often a dangerous practice for those students who are reading under sixth-grade level, whether retarded in reading or not. Such reading encourages the habit of skipping or skimming in place of careful reading and understanding. Consequently, any emphasis upon speed, except through the practices mentioned in the preceding paragraph, is not usual in the elementary school. It is better left to the secondary school, except for seventh and eighth graders reading on or above grade level and gifted students reading above sixth-grade level.

If teaching speeded reading is attempted, it is important to keep in mind that *speed in itself has no value.* Speed of understanding, or "rate of comprehension," is the proper concept. A rate of reading that is ideal for some purposes and with some materials may be completely inappropriate for other purposes and materials. Able readers are adaptable and versatile; they are able to change their rate of reading so that they achieve the understanding suitable to their purposes and to the difficulty of the material. Such maturity in reading is not achieved immediately and the elementary school can only begin such training. (It is now recognized that secondary schools and colleges must also teach some reading.)

Efficient eye movements, few and short fixation pauses, and a good return sweep to the next line are *symptoms* of good reading. However, a person may not necessarily become a good reader by developing eye movements, longer perception spans, or faster perceptions. Using a machine that increases perception span may help a person to see more at one fixation, but unless provision is made for transfer of the skill to the printed page, the increased perception span may have no practical purpose. A mechanistic approach by itself will not ordinarily result in lasting gains, but as part of a program with older pupils, the machine may act as a motivating device or as proof to the student of her or his own potential. A machine technique should approximate natural reading insofar as possible.

To a great extent, after basic skills are mastered, rate of reading is related to rate of thinking. Children read as fast as they can assimilate ideas if there are no problems with the foundation skills. This is why the gifted youngster may need earlier instruction in improving his or her reading speed.

## Principles and Techniques for Improving Reading Rate

able 4.4 lists some specific techniques which can help students increase eir rate of comprehension. But there are some general principles underlying ine techniques that should be discussed first.

To begin with, it is important that the learner be performing smoothly and correctly on the material used before trying to develop speed. Therefore, it is best for the teacher to use easier material for speeded practice—material at least two years below the reading level of regular work. It is also important that unknown words or completely new concepts be excluded from the speeded reading exercise.

If the equipment is available, some tachistoscopic practice and controlled or paced reading on machines should be included. However, major emphasis should remain on comprehension. What the reader should be striving for is increased mental alertness and ability to see thought units rather than single words.

In this respect, teachers should help students understand that reading speed is relative. It is not measured in words per minute or by how fast other students read. Rather, progress is measured by how much a reader's active understanding—how much he or she gives to, not takes from, the reading— increases over a period of time. Graphs and charts should be kept by each individual to show his or her daily progress.

Various materials should be used both to keep interest level high and to show that speed can vary depending on the reader's purpose. However, comprehension should always be checked. Speed should not count unless comprehension is at a predetermined level of adequacy (usually 75 percent). Comprehension is so important that its improvement should be worked on at least as often as speed. Drills should be very short so that attention can remain at maximum. And checks should deemphasize recall of details in favor of general understanding. If no progress is evident over a period of time, vision and other physical factors that could cause problems in rapid perception should be checked.

For specific activities that can implement these general principles, consult the table below.

## TABLE 4.4 METHODS FOR IMPROVING RATE OF READING

| Objective | Procedures | References and Materials |
|---|---|---|
| To eliminate lip movement and vocalization. | Have pupils place their fingers over their lips or on the sides of their throat, or grip a pencil | |

| Objective | Procedures | References and Materials |
|---|---|---|
| | between the teeth and against the tongue. | |
| | Use phrases on flash cards or filmstrips with phrases and stories rather than single words. | Dolch, E. W. "Sight Phrase Cards." Champaign, Ill.: Garrard. |
| | Eliminate finger pointing. | Use a marker and gradually have the student discard it. |
| | Place emphasis on thoughts rather than words. Use tachistoscopic exercises requiring answers that emphasize content rather than the return of exact words. | For information on tachistoscopes and their use, see Barnette, Gasper. *Learning Through Seeing with Tachistoscopic Techniques.* Sunland, Calif.: Learning Through Seeing. |
| | Use material that is very easy, especially stories with suspense. | |
| To eliminate regressions | Use mechanical pacing devices. | SRA Reading Accelerator. Chicago: Science Research Associates. |
| | Use a "cover card," a 5″ x 8″ card which the student moves down the page as he or she reads, covering what has already been read. | |
| | Discuss the proper time for regression. Rereading should occur only when the paragraph has been completed and the reader has not found a main idea. | |
| To teach the habit of more complete atten- | Use very short selections but be sure that compre- | "Rate Builders," in the *SRA Reading Labora-* |

| Objective | Procedures | References and Materials |
|-----------|-----------|------------------------|
| tion to the reading task | hension is always checked. | *tories.* Chicago: Science Research Associates. |
| | Use a projection device that gives a complete story. | *Controlled Reader.* Huntington, N.Y.: Educational Development Laboratories. |
| | Ditto materials that are short, and which you have found to be interesting to this age group. Be sure you have questions and set the purposes before reading. | |
| To show the difference in attack for differing materials | Vary the difficulty level of speed drills. Emphasize the difference to students. Have them estimate the different speed they might achieve if the level is lowered three grades in difficulty; then have them attempt to attain or better their estimate without any problems in comprehension. | Ditto materials from various sources. Rewrite some to different levels of difficulty. Code so that you know the difficulty level of each. |
| | Give exercises in locating information quickly by the use of such ideas as chapter headings, subheads, key words, italics. | |
| | Encourage wide, easy reading for pleasure requiring no book report. An indication of title, author, and one line or two of written reaction is sufficient. | Trade books in great variety. Also, *SRA Pilot Library.* Chicago: Science Research Associates; and *Literature Sampler* and *Literature Sampler Junior.* New York: Xerox Educational Division. |

Other references giving discussions of rate of reading which include methods and materials are:

Aukerman, Robert C. *Reading in the Secondary School Classroom*. New York: McGraw-Hill, 1972, pp. 289–302.
Dallmann, Martha, et al. *The Teaching of Reading*. 4th ed. New York: Holt, Rinehart & Winston, 1974. Chapters 7A and 7B.
Figurel, J. Allen, ed. *Changing Concepts of Reading Instruction*. Newark, Del.: International Reading Association, 1961, pp. 214–30.
Heilman, Arthur W. *Principles and Practices of Teaching Reading*. 2nd ed. Columbus, Ohio: Charles E. Merrill, 1967, pp. 388–92.

## VOCABULARY

Children have several vocabularies: listening vocabulary, reading vocabulary, speaking vocabulary, and writing vocabulary. These change in importance and use with age. The first vocabulary acquired is the listening vocabulary, the words that children are able to understand when they hear them. Gradually, the speaking vocabulary grows to include almost all the listening vocabulary, though it probably never really reaches it. Usually reading and writing vocabularies are nonexistent until after children enter school. The reading vocabulary is built upon the listening and speaking vocabulary. Since getting the meaning is an important part of reading, children cannot really read a word until they understand it from having had experience with it in listening and speaking. Reading vocabulary usually overtakes speaking vocabulary somewhere in the intermediate grades but in many cases does not exceed the listening vocabulary. There are, however, many individual cases in which children can understand words that they cannot pronounce, since they have never heard nor spoken them. The writing vocabulary is the last to form, needing the other three for a foundation. It usually remains the smallest of all, partially because of the difficulty of spelling.

This progression, from listening to speaking to reading to writing, is quite important in teaching. Taking shortcuts will usually lead to incomplete understanding. Research findings indicate that vocabulary develops rapidly before children enter school, slows down somewhat during the third and fourth years of school, and drops off from that point. At least two interpretations are possible: (1) the school situation may be such that vocabulary growth tends to be impeded; or (2) teachers may be interfering with the normal developmental sequence in the acquisition of meaning vocabulary.

Teachers should be aware of the value of building vocabulary with both breadth and depth of meaning. It is also important to realize the personal factor in symbols—denotative meanings may be fairly precise, but connotative meanings are often quite personal. Robert McCracken has argued that students need to understand the various ways words function.[1] They should be aware that words such as "democracy" summarize ideas, words like "tree" denote, words like "amble" express movement, words like "stealthily" generate an emotional response, words like "home" elicit images, and so forth. They need to realize that they as readers play a significant role in giving meaning to words that they read.

Teachers can use word lists to add both breadth and depth to students' vocabulary. The following standard word lists give the most common or the most useful words in reading, spelling, and writing:

Buckingham, B. R., and Dolch, E. W. *A Combined Word List.* Boston: Ginn, 1936. Although this is an older list, it is still very valuable. It shows the grade level and frequency of word use in ten different studies of vocabulary.

Durrell, Donald D. *Improving Reading Instruction.* New York: Harcourt, Brace & World. 1956. Two word lists are included in the appendix to this book. The first, "Remedial Reading Vocabulary for Primary Grades," gives 754 words in seven frequency levels. The second is a list of words useful in grades four, five, and six taken from word counts of books frequently used in these grades. About 600 to 800 words are given for each grade.

Harris, Albert J., and Jacobson, Milton D. *Basic Elementary Reading Vocabularies.* New York: Macmillan, 1972. This very recent listing is based on the vocabulary of sixteen basal reader series in the first six grades. There are actually two major listings—one shows the most frequently used words and a second arranges the words in difficulty levels from preprimer through sixth grades.

Horn, Ernest. *A Basic Writing Vocabulary.* University of Iowa Monographs in Education, No. 4. Iowa City, Iowa: University of Iowa, 1926. Though old, this book is still applicable. It gives 10,000 words most likely to be written by adults and should, therefore, be learned by older children in reading and spelling.

Rinsland, Henry. *A Basic Vocabulary of Elementary School Children.* New York: Macmillan, 1945. This contains over 25,000 words based on word counts of children's writing in grades one to eight. It also shows the frequency of use of the words by grades.

Thorndike, Edward L., and Lorge, Irving. *Teacher's Word Book of 30,000 Words.* New York: Teachers College, Columbia University, 1944. Words are listed in terms of their frequency of appearance per 1 million and 4 million running words in magazines, juvenile books, and semantic counts.

---

[1] "The Development of Reading Vocabulary in the Junior High School," Reading Bulletin, No. 105 (Boston: Allyn & Bacon). (Free brochure.)

## Practices for Developing Vocabulary

In expanding students' vocabularies, teachers should keep in mind the importance of attaching student experiences to new words. Students often have familiarity with new words through their experience but are unable to make the connection until they are encouraged to speak or write about it. Even if particular students have no such personal experience to attach, they can learn a great deal from other students who have and are willing to share it. Of course, besides firsthand experience, students can still find meaning in new words vicariously through their reading. As long as the context is understandable and the new word is repeated, it may be added to the vocabulary of the reader (though pronunciation may be a problem).

There are many other ways for children to gain a wider exposure to words. Sometimes the analysis of the meaning of word parts—Latin and Greek prefixes, suffixes, and roots—is useful (though children should be made aware that English usage sometimes changes meaning and spelling). Bright children especially like to explore the origins of English words, and this may become the basis for a self-perpetuating type of study.

Finally, many situations arise in the classroom where variant meanings of a common word come up. Drawing student attention to the common core of meaning and how the present variant affects that core meaning can be helpful. For complete word knowledge, students need such study.

A few more specific suggestions for the development of reading vocabulary follow in Table 4.5. For teachers working at seventh- and eighth-grade levels, the methods and materials given in Chapter 5 may be more applicable.

## TABLE 4.5 METHODS OF DEVELOPING VOCABULARY

| Objective | Procedures | References and Materials |
|---|---|---|
| To broaden experiences with words | Look at motion pictures, photographs, cartoons, maps, paintings, and so forth, and then *discuss* them. | Tinker, Miles A., and McCullough, Constance M. *Teaching Elementary Reading.* New York: Appleton-Century-Crofts, 1968. |
| | Listen to radio or educational TV, to reading by the teacher, to experiences of classmates, to speakers from the community. | McCullough, Constance M. "Independent Reading Activities." (New York: Ginn). (Free bulletin.) |
| | Discuss historical points of interest after excursions. | Strang, Ruth, McCullough, Constance M., and Traxler, Arthur. |

| Objective | Procedures | References and Materials |
|---|---|---|
| | Cut out some small pictures from magazines or old books. Prepare a set of cards with a sentence on each card, describing one of the pictures. Put the pictures and sentences in an envelope or box. Children match the sentence with the picture. | *The Improvement of Reading.* 4th ed. New York: McGraw-Hill, 1967, pp. 238–49. |
| | Have children explain an author's choice of one word over another. | |
| To encourage students to use words | Have pupils match a list of words with a random list of synonyms, definitions, or opposites; or list words and have pupils supply synonyms, definitions, or opposites. | |
| | Provide sentences with certain words underlined. Have students determine the meaning from context and then use the dictionary to check their work. Discussions may arise about common meanings or multiple meanings. | |
| | Have students use homonyms in sentences or fill in blanks by choosing between two homonyms. | Guides to basal readers. |
| | Use games and self-checking exercises: Scrabble, prefix and suffix word wheels, *Spelling Laboratory* wheels, etc. | *Spelling Laboratory.* Chicago: Science Research Associates. |
| To teach about special kinds of words | Read a poem with vivid imagery. Have children | Arbuthnot, May H., and Root, Shelton L. |

| Objective | Procedures | References and Materials |
|-----------|------------|--------------------------|
|  | illustrate and write a sentence about the picture or poem. | *Time for Poetry*. Chicago: Scott, Foresman, 1968. |
|  | On designated pages of the reader, ask pupils to find action words. Have them tell what these words make them see. | Supplementary readers |
|  | Figures of speech are especially difficult to understand. Give parts of sentences. Have children fill in the correct letter of the completing part, or use strips and a pocket chart or the chalk tray. For example: | Can be done with duplicating masters or by using oak tag strips. |
|  | 1. The shining back of the tuna was —— <br> 2. The big tuna lurched about —— <br> 3. The blue waters of the cove sparkled —— <br> 4. Rain pattering on the window sounded —— <br>  a. like a ship in a storm. <br>  b. like tiny tapping fingers. <br>  c. like polished silver. <br>  d. like jewels. | *Interesting Origins of English Words*. Springfield, Mass.: G. & C. Merriam. |
|  | Whenever a word is met in a content area where that word has a special meaning different from its common meaning, call this difference to the attention of pupils. |  |

Many other suggestions are available in:

Harris, Albert J. *How to Increase Reading Ability*. New York: David McKay, 1961, pp. 396–421.

Hildreth, Gertrude. *Teaching Reading*. New York: Holt, Rinehart & Winston, 1958, pp. 489–502.

Schubert, Delwyn G., and Torgerson, Theodore L. *Improving the Reading Program*. 3rd ed. Dubuque, Iowa: William C. Brown, 1972, pp. 240–45.

Zintz, Miles V. *Corrective Reading*. 2nd ed. Dubuque, Iowa: William C. Brown, 1972, pp. 401–02.

## STUDY SKILLS

A good basal reading program develops most of the study skills at various levels. The following list of suggestions, therefore, is not intended to be complete or to cover all possible areas; it is merely indicative of techniques that may be used in the development of study skills.

1.   Help students use the table of contents to locate a story in a reader or in other sources. Ask such questions as, "Who wrote the story or article? Where does the story begin? Which chapter begins on page 35?"

2.   Refer to the index in books to locate materials for committees, interest groups, or classes. Make up exercises in how to use the index.

3.   Help children to notice publication dates of materials. Help them also to take note of authors and attempt to learn something about them.

4.   Use the telephone book in class to look up numbers; use bus schedules or plane schedules to develop this special kind of locational skill.

5.   Point out book arrangements in the library.

6.   Show pupils how to use section titles and subheadings to assist in locating main ideas.

7.   Have pupils search various materials on a given topic, selecting those that are relevant and rejecting those that are irrelevant.

8.   Let pupils examine current materials such as newspapers for the validity of stated or implied points of view.

9.   Review or teach the use of the card catalog and how to locate books for reference by numerical categories. Teach pupils to search under several related subject headings for a book or desired information.

10.   Introduce Roget's *Thesaurus* and its uses. (For an introductory thesaurus, try: Treanor, John H. *A First Thesaurus*. Cambridge, Mass.: Educators Publishing Service, 1961.)

11.   Introduce sources such as *Who's Who*, the *World Almanac*, the *Dictionary of American Biography*, *Pageant of America*, various unabridged dictionaries and encyclopedias, and *Reader's Guide to Periodical Literature*.

12.   Have students make charts and graphs from information found in other forms.

13.   Help pupils to detect meaning changes brought about by punctuation.

14.   Develop standards, with the students, for selecting materials to read.

15.   Have pupils take notes in science or social studies (on field trips or during interviews with resource people, for example), for oral and written reports.

16.   Review the following (and teach if necessary): table of contents, index, glossary, preface, copyright date, title page, appendix, footnotes.

17.   Have pupils do a cooperative outline on the board. Show them how to use primary headings, subheadings, italics, and so forth as cues.

18.   Use the "Listening Skill Builders" in the *SRA Reading Laboratory*. Chicago: Science Research Associates.

19.   Teach SQ3R method of study, or use the adaptation of this method as given in the *SRA Reading Laboratory*:

    *S*:   Survey—see what is coming—take an overview of the section.

    *Q*:   Raise questions that can be answered by the passage. Turn the section heading into a question.

    *R*:   Read to answer the above question in the section.

    *R*:   Review to see whether answers are correct.

    *R*:   Recite material in the form likely to be used later.

20.   Do some direct teaching of the factors that aid in study, such as:

    a.   Having a clear purpose or goal

    b.   Having a regular place to study—quiet with good lighting

    c.   Having a regular time for study—early, before becoming fatigued

    d.   Having the necessary equipment ready before beginning work

    e.   Starting without dawdling

    f.   Using the techniques of study taught in the classroom

    g.   Completing the assignment, being conscious of the assignment, its due date, its requirements, and so forth

For further reference, see:

Bamman, Henry A., et al. *Fundamentals of Basic Reading Instruction*. New York: David McKay, 1973. Chapter 14.

Heilman, Arthur. *Principles and Practices of Teaching Reading*. 2nd ed. Columbus, Ohio: Charles E. Merrill, 1967, pp. 371–96.

Strang, Ruth, McCullough, Constance, and Traxler, Arthur. *The Improvement of Reading*. 4th ed. New York: McGraw-Hill, 1967, pp. 265–68.

# 5 INTERESTS AND ATTITUDES

It does little good to teach a child *how* to read if he or she does not *want* to read. Few adults read widely after leaving school. This may be, at least in part, a consequence of being required to read large amounts of uninteresting material in school, resulting in a desire for escape from reading afterward. The area of interests and attitudes, therefore, is a highly important one for teachers to understand. Working for positive improvement there can have lifelong effects.

## INTERESTS

The effects of interest in specific reading materials are obvious in both the classroom and in daily life. Students respond more fully to passages in which they are more interested. In fact, pupils are able to read materials in their field of interest that are comparatively more difficult when judged by such criteria as vocabulary difficulty and sentence structure.

Reading interest is the result of a personal interaction between the individual and the reading material. There are important moments in the development of an individual when a certain book has tremendous value and appeal. Reading interests and overall life interests are highly related. A person reading a letter from a loved one is fully involved, growing sensitive to context, ambiguity, implications, and even punctuation as never before. This example may show better than any research the relation between interest and reading skill. Therefore, reading interests should be studied directly and used in the classroom to give direction, purpose, and satisfaction.

This does not mean that teachers should permit students to become permanently stopped at a low level of preference or that they should not attempt to develop discriminating tastes in reading. New and varied interests can and should be built, but they are built more often through successful experiences with materials of present interest that gradually introduce new taste and discrimination. Variation is more likely to evolve gradually from pleasurable experience concerned with a present need of the individual than from forced change.

*Methods of Ascertaining Interests*

Interests vary in kind, diversity and intensity. To a great extent, they are products of factors such as intelligence, general maturity, home background, previous experience, and location, as those factors operate in the personality and perceptions of the individual.

There are a number of different ways to measure interests. The most frequently used indicators are:

1. *Expressions of interest.* These may be oral or written statements of interest in an activity, occupation, or area of competency.

2. *Manifestations of interest.* Observed activities in which the behavior reveals trends of interest patterns. Absence of specific interests may also be used as a guide.

3. *Tests of interest.* There are really no true tests of interest available, though the technique of using vocabulary tests as interest tests has been studied. Other approaches through attention and memory are possible.

4. *Inventories of interest patterns.* These have been studied extensively. Inventories measure interest by having the individual react to a varied number of statements or possible preferences.

Of these methods, the last seems to offer the best possibilities with older pupils. If the person has developed sufficient maturity through experiences, the indications shown by the standardized pattern of the interest inventory are more likely to persist than are momentary indications on a questionnaire or spur-of-the-moment expressions.

With younger children, the discovery of interests through observation of students during classroom work and extracurricular activities may work well, particularly in a self-contained classroom. However, observing a large number of students in a rather structured classroom situation, as in most secondary schools, presents a real problem. Actually, to do it well, the teacher should keep an anecdotal record of observations of the student in as many situations as possible so that some synthesis pointing toward interests can be made. Ordinarily this cannot be done beyond elementary school.

Since the more formal methods of determining student interests—checklists, questionnaires, and interest inventories—require more technical knowledge to use them effectively, we will discuss them more thoroughly below.

**Checklists and questionnaires.** Checklists and questionnaires may be used easily with students, especially with those that appear to have ability but lack motivation or achievement. It is quite possible, however, for students to fill in blanks on such instruments in order to conform with what is being asked of them and not because of any real or abiding interest in the material. Questionnaires usually leave more room for individual response than do checklists, and can be more valuable because of the particular clues given. In addition, if a short interview can be arranged using the questionnaire as a basis, some probing is possible to obtain information otherwise unobtainable.

For samples of checklists and questionnaires, see:

Austin, M. C., Bush, C. L., and Huebner, M. H. *Reading Evaluation.* New York: The Ronald Press, 1961.

Bamman, H. A., Dawson, M. A., and McGovern, J. J. *Fundamentals of Basic Reading Instruction.* 3rd ed. New York: David McKay, 1973.

Harris, Albert J. *How to Increase Reading Ability.* 5th ed. New York: David McKay, 1970.

Jewett, Arno, ed. *Improving Reading in the Junior High School.* Bulletin 1957, No. 10. Washington: U.S. Government Printing Office, 1957.

Strang, Ruth. *Diagnostic Teaching of Reading.* 2nd ed. New York: McGraw-Hill, 1968.

Witty, Paul. *Reading in Modern Education.* Boston: D. C. Heath, 1949.

**Interest inventories.** For most students in the secondary school, the use of the interest inventory provides standardized information, takes little time on the part of teachers and students, and shows patterns which are often valuable. Two purposes may be served—planning course work and planning sensibly toward a later vocational choice. Both involve present school course choices and are therefore related to advising and counseling. But the results can be used as well to discover patterns of interest for reading. Several interest inventories are in wide use at the present time.

The *Kuder Preference Record, Vocational Form C*, compiled by G. Frederic Kuder (Chicago: Science Research Associates), consists of a large number of items, each listing three activities. The student indicates which activity of the three he or she likes most and which least. A machine-scoring answer sheet may be used (Form CM), or a self-scoring pin punchtype answer pad is available that requires only the counting of responses (Form CH). After scoring, a profile of preference scores may be plotted in areas involving outdoor, mechanical, computational, scientific, persuasive, artistic, literary, musical, social service, and clerical activities. A V-score (verfication) is also given and serves to indicate inconsistent responses which contribute to doubtful profiles. Much information is available in the manual accompanying the inventory, and the Kuder Book List (described in the next section) may be obtained to accompany the inventory and help in the use of the results by directing the student to books that are available in his or her areas of interest.

Edward K. Strong, Jr.'s *Vocational Interest Blank for Men* and *Vocational Interest Blank for Women* (Stanford, Calif.: Stanford University Press) have scoring scales comparing the individual's answers to those of successful adults in a large number of different occupational groups and specific occupations. These are especially useful for college-bound students but are probably best administered near the end of high school. Scores are expressed in letter grades. Scoring services are offered, but scoring by hand is possible though extremely laborious. Special scales (interest maturity, occupational level, and masculinity-femininity) are available for use by trained counselors.

The *Occupational Interest Inventory* of Edwin Lee and Louis Thorpe (Monterey, Calif.: California Test Bureau) tests for fields of interest labeled as personal-social, natural, mechanical, business, the arts, and the sciences. In addition, three more general types of interest are surveyed—verbal, manipulative, and computational—and a score for level of interest is given. The reading difficulty level of the inventory is quite low, probably averaging below the seventh-grade level. Answers may be either hand- or machine-scored. An interest analysis report is available so that scores may be interpreted to students and parents. The intermediate form is for grade seven through adult; the advanced form for grade nine through adult.

The *SRA Youth Inventory*, compiled by H. H. Remmers, A. J. Drucker, and Benjamin Shimberg (Chicago: Science Research Associates) asks students to indicate their problems in areas labeled *My School, Looking Ahead, About Myself, Getting Along with Others, My Home and Family, Boy Meets Girl, Health,* and *Things in General.* Designed for use in grades nine through twelve, this inventory is not strictly an interest inventory, but the teacher may discover clues so that reading selections related to problem areas may be suggested. Therefore, it serves more as an indication for bibliotherapy than as an interest inventory. In terms of reading interests, however, it may accomplish just as much direction.

Finally, K. P. Weingarten's *Picture Interest Inventory* (Monterey, Calif.: California Test Bureau) invites students' responses to a series of sketches of activities having occupational significance. It is a new inventory and may be used from grade seven up, regardless of reading or writing ability or language comprehension. The scores are in the areas of interpersonal service, natural (outdoor), mechanical, business, esthetic, scientific, verbal activities, computational activities, and time perspective. Directions are read by the examiner; answers are recorded on either machine- or hand-scored answer sheets, the latter of which are scored with stencils. This inventory should prove of real value in remedial reading classes.

Scores indicating interest, preference, or problem areas on any of the above may be counted and profiled by the students if administered in the classroom. Since there are no right or wrong answers, and since most students tend to score high in at least one area of the test, there is no problem, but rather real value, in having a student score and profile his or her own test.

### Finding Interesting Books To Fit

After the interest profile has been completed by whatever means, it is time to direct these findings into reading materials. One of the best methods of accomplishing this is through a book list organized by interest areas and levels of difficulty.

If an inventory has been used, the book list should contain the same areas of interest as the inventory, so that the transfer is direct. Each interest area should show easy, average, and difficult books, so labeled. Teachers should enlist the aid of the librarian in making up these lists, which can consist simply of titles for further investigation or can contain brief annotations. Book lists that are classified according to area of interest and difficulty are very helpful.[1]

A commercially available book list is designed to fit the *Kuder Preference Record*.[2] It shows the interest profile on the cover, has a page explaining the profiled interests, and contains several pages of book lists arranged according to the ten interest areas and at three difficulty levels.

Exhibits of books by interest area may be set up in the classroom, or shelves labeled by interest and difficulty may be stocked with books suggested on the lists. Availability is essential because a visit to the library is sometimes discouraging for a student who reads little and finds it difficult to locate what is wanted.

For the pupil who always reads one type of story and does not seem to realize that there are other things, "My Reading Design"[3] can prove helpful. It is a circular graph of books read, recorded by types, and serves to emphasize over-concentration in one area.

Throughout this section on interests, the older student has been emphasized, primarily because (1) it is possible to use more evaluatory instruments with the secondary student; and (2) interest information regarding individuals is more likely to be lacking at that level. However, the conclusions shown here apply almost equally well to younger pupils, and certainly the effect of interest is equally important.

## ATTITUDES

Attitudes may be defined as predispositions to act either favorably or unfavorably toward some group, institution, situation, or object. They are, of course, highly related to interests but tend to be thought of as broader and more generalized feelings, often not particularly conscious, but most certainly affecting individual behavior.

### Attitude Measurement

As with interests, attitudes may be detected to some degree through oral or written expressions of the individual, or by observing behaviors which indi-

[1] See, for example, George Spache, *Good Reading for Poor Readers* (Champaign, Ill.: Garrard, revised every two years).

[2] G. Frederic Kuder, *Kuder Book List* (Chicago: Science Research Associates).

[3] G. O. Simpson, "My Reading Design" (Defiance, Ohio: The Hubbard Company, 1962).

cate attitudes. However, since individuals may have feelings inconsistent with the ways they behave, the validity of observational techniques and of overt expressions is questionable. As a consequence, various types of attitude scales have been developed, some cleverly disguised so the examinee believes he or she is responding to an informational, perception, or judgment test. The questions, however, have either equally incorrect answers or no known answers, and the responses show attitude rather than knowledge.

For information on attitude scales, consult:

Fishbein, Martin, ed. *Readings in Attitude Theory and Measurement.* New York: John Wiley & Sons, 1967.

Sax, Gilbert. *Principles of Educational Measurement and Evaluation.* Belmont, Calif.: Wadsworth, 1974.

Shaw, Marvin E., and Wright, Jack M. *Scales for the Measurement of Attitudes.* New York: McGraw-Hill, 1967.

Without going into the technical aspects of attitude measurement, a teacher may discover a great deal from student responses to reading autobiographies (in either questionnaire or essay form), or by utilizing a sentence completion form. For example, such questions as the following may be employed:

When I am asked to read, I _____.

To me, books _____.

I'd read more if_____.

What I like to do best in my spare time is _____.

The most exciting ideas to me are _____.

I want adults to understand that _____.

Most of my attention in school is _____.

I think the best thing in school is _____.

Questions like these should be answered rapidly with the first thing that comes to mind, and it should be emphasized that there are no incorrect answers. Further examples may be found in:

Strang, Ruth. *Diagnostic Teaching of Reading.* 2nd ed. New York: McGraw-Hill, 1968.

Strang, Ruth, McCullough, Constance M., and Traxler, Arthur. *The Improvement of Reading.* 4th ed. New York: McGraw-Hill, 1967.

Many student attitudes may be discovered, of course, through conferences. Often, in the more private situation, reasons for feelings of inadequacy or particular preferences are voiced which would not show in the group or which would not be written down in the questionnaire. In such instances, the teacher should be careful not to judge, accepting rather than reacting to the attitudes shown.

### The Effect of School Practices

Many pupil attitudes about school and books are produced rather directly by school practices. Three areas in particular are especially important in attitude development—school marks, homework, and encouragement provided the poor reader. Often, heightened teacher awareness in these areas may do a great deal for attitudes without any pupil diagnosis.

**School marks and teacher's evaluations.** A competent teacher appraises the progress of a student in relation to repeated experiences with that student in the classroom. Tests are not the only measures used to determine progress and amount of learning. The teacher examines the reading skills of the student as a part of the performance of the individual, and grades given will reflect this to some degree. However, whenever there is an emphasis on content, grades in school are more likely to show the relative standing of a student in comparison with peers. These grades do not, to any great degree, reflect the potential the individual *may* have, or how much he or she may have *progressed* during the course in a skill area of development such as reading.

If a pupil is a relatively poor reader and is given pencil-and-paper tests or writing tasks to do for the evaluation, his or her knowledge about the subject will not show up. Since writing follows reading as a skill, he or she will be unable to demonstrate growing knowledge and may be getting a failing grade simply on the basis of lack of communication skill rather than lack of information. Often this can be a cause of failure feelings, even though the student does not actually fail to achieve the objectives of the content course, and can eventually lead to dropping out of school.

There is also the problem of the variability and reliability of a teacher's grades. Studies show that girls tend to receive higher grades than boys for the same level of achievement, that well-liked students are marked higher than less-liked students, and that students in the center of the distribution tend to be marked on a chance basis. In addition, most teachers differ in their interpretation of achievement, so that the value of a given grade differs from class to class and from school to school. Such factors as written work, oral discussion, kind of examination given, attitude, homework, and classwork are weighted differently by different teachers.

In general, then, teachers' marks should not be considered to any great extent in reading diagnosis, except that each teacher should be conscious of those who are laboring under a skill deficiency. Though the marks do not provide a true index to potential, they may provide a clue to type of difficulty.

For more discussion of these points, see:

Harris, Chester W. ed. *Encyclopedia of Educational Research.* 3rd ed. New York: Macmillan, 1960.

**Homework?**    When assigning work to be done at home, the teacher should consider:

1.  If the pupil has difficulty in reading, is there anyone at home who will (or can) help? Any child will dread the feeling of stupidity in front of parents if the parents happen to be academically able themselves. And if the parents did not go very far in school themselves, they may be completely unable to help.

2.  Does each individual really know what is expected of him or her on the homework? Has the teacher set the exact purposes for the reading, or are the students simply supposed to move their eyes over so many pages of print, hoping somehow to "get" the right thing?

3.  Has the class been prepared for the reading by reviewing related facts, helping to clarify concepts that will be encountered, giving advance information on new vocabulary, and so forth?

4.  Is this a task that is simply further practice on an understood matter in order to perfect the skill, or is supervision during study essential to ensure that mistakes will not be practiced?

5.  Will doing this job at home tonight add to what happens in class tomorrow, or detract from it? Will any possible excitement be killed by the repetition? Will most of the class do the assignment or wait for the teacher to go over it for them? Or will only those who are already feeling too much pressure attempt this task too?

Much assigned homework is wasted effort and poor preparation for the classroom learning situation. The practice may be geared more to making facts permanent than to making skills perfect. In general, carefully supervised study in the room will accomplish much more in less time. The teacher is there to teach each student as an individual and meet problems in the lesson as they arise. In a classroom situation, a teacher can evaluate the learning and the common difficulties much sooner and better.

**Encouraging the poor reader to try.**    No one deliberately asks for failure. The poor reader will seldom use "leisure" time for reading; other activities provide more relaxation and less work. For such a reader, there is little fun in struggling through a book, and he or she may refuse to do more than the absolute minimum of required reading, if that. Many of these students have never finished a single book.

Exhorting poor readers to do more reading will only make them transfer their difficulty in reading to difficulty with teachers. Teachers should not become discouraged if most attempts to encourage reading for information or pleasure are met with complete indifference or definite objection. The following practices may help to lessen student resistance to reading.

Accept *any* book as being worthwhile to the reader who completes it.

Accept *any* review of reading, including individual reports to the teacher, panel discussions, short reactions, a checklist report.

Have available in the classroom books that are as easy and interesting to read as possible. Allow students to keep them at home for relatively long periods of time. (Most poor readers are frightened by libraries.)

Have students recommend books to each other. Most poor readers will trust the judgment of their peers more than they will that of the teacher.

Be available to define unknown words or to give guidance in finding the meaning. Never suggest that the reader should already know the word.

Set aside some class time for free reading. (For use of the sustained silent reading approach, see McCracken below.)

Avoid comparisons between students as to the amount and quality of reading done.

Have available for self-help programmed booklets to review or teach skills.

For more motivational ideas, see:

George, Mary Yanaga. *Language Art: An Ideabook.* Scranton, Pa.: Intext, 1970.

McCracken, Robert A., and McCracken, Marlene J. *Reading Is Only the Tiger's Tail.* San Rafael, Calif.: Leswing Press, 1972.

Spache, Evelyn B. *Reading Activities for Child Involvement.* Boston: Allyn & Bacon, 1972.

# 6 HELPING THE DISABLED READER

The poor reader has always been present in the schools, and probably there will always be some children who for a number of reasons cannot learn to read as well as the majority of their peers. Determining causes of poor reading, locating pupils who could be helped, and selecting methods for helping these pupils have always posed questions for elementary school administrators and teachers.

Several books and numerous articles have described the facts and understandings available in regard to reading disability, but few educators have the time to read and to digest all of this information. Each section in this chapter gives a summary and also refers the reader to various sources if more information is desired.

## GENERAL TYPES OF READING PROBLEM CASES

There are many ways of categorizing reading problems, or typing children who are experiencing difficulty in learning to read. Rather than attempt to treat all categories in depth, this section will briefly characterize the more typical students meeting reading difficulty.

### Readers with Feelings of Inadequacy

Older students with a severe reading difficulty often suffer from a deep sense of inadequacy. In their own eyes and in the eyes of others, they have been failures in school for several years. They may already have suffered disappointment because special help provided in the lower grades did not solve the problem. They may have been rejected by peers or parents. There may have been cruel laughter at their best attempts and at consistently poor grades. Because of these unhappy past experiences, such students may be incapable of finding pleasure in any kind of reading at their interest level, and they may be discipline problems besides. For these reasons, the longer poor reading habits have existed, the more difficult they are to overcome. The pupils are sure that they are "dumb," they do not wish to place themselves in situations that invite more failure, and they tend to "fight the system."

It is easy to interpret such reactions as a total lack of interest in learning. But hardly ever is this the case; rather, the students have set up a protective screen. Most older poor readers desire help very much but would like to avoid public advertisement of the seriousness of their problem. And most of these reading difficulties are amenable to help given properly.

### Readers with Restricted Mental Abilities

Pupils with low capacity for learning usually have an overall weakness in reading skills. Their reading comprehension score ordinarily will be lower than their word-recognition skills would suggest. Their oral reading may be comparatively good but without much expression, and word-attack skills (particularly more complex ones such as digraphs, diphthongs, and syllabication) may raise problems for them. Their understanding of words, both spoken and written, is limited, and spelling and arithmetic skills are also likely to be at a low level. Very seldom will special help for this type of reader bring about a marked improvement, since in most cases they will be reading as well as they can.

Occasionally the above pattern will be demonstrated by pupils from a disadvantaged background. In this case they may quite often be helped, since the deciding factor is more likely to be paucity of background rather than limitations in native intelligence. Intelligence, as measured by tests, actually can be increased in such cases; this improvement in basic thinking skills (such as language facility) then will be reflected in improved reading skill— *if they are taught.*

### Readers with Good Mental Abilities but with Specific Problems

Poor readers whose intellectual level is higher than their reading level will develop a different pattern of learning. On tests they will usually score higher on reading comprehension than on word recognition. Their skill in oral reading will be poor, often considerably lower than their silent reading comprehension. Word-attack skills are likely to be partially or wholly absent because they lack training in these areas (or more often, they do not remember the training). Their vocabulary and listening comprehension will be relatively good, but problems in spelling, handwriting, and grammar may interfere with their written answers to questions. Their skill in computation is good, although arithmetic problems that require reading will be difficult for them. Such students are good prospects for remediation. The areas for remediation are described more fully below.

**Difficulty in word recognition.**   Pupils with this problem may be able to read only a few words either because their sight vocabulary is poor or because they lack a knowledge of the shorter, basic words. Common problems are mispronunciation or miscalling of words, reversals of letters or words, hesitation, and repetition. These last two indicate an insecurity about word knowledge. The students' level of reading and the number of words they know will determine the level of materials that can be used with them.

Often, of late, this reading problem has been given the medical diagnosis of dyslexia. In the main this means that the child is not up to his or her potential as a reader, exhibits reversals of words and letters, and has severe difficulty in visual perception. Dyslexia is generally neither uncorrectable nor permanent.

**Weakness in word attack.**   The reading level may vary to an even greater degree when word-attack skills are weak. Students reading at grade level may still have trouble in attacking new words. They may not know the common sounds of vowels, consonants, digraphs, diphthongs, and blends. They may not have mastered the pronunciations of structural endings or common prefixes. Syllabication and using the dictionary may be problems for them. At the opposite extreme, there are students who know phonics fairly well but who still cannot read with any ease. There are some who can give all the isolated sounds of vowels and consonants but who cannot put them together to read, even at a slow rate. The kind of remediation needed, therefore, will depend on the skill or skills that students need to develop. The learning sequence and the reading level at which the skill is to be presented will have to be considered.

**Limited vocabulary.**   As a rule, poor readers with good intellectual ability have a much higher listening vocabulary than reading vocabulary. Occasionally, however, a meager verbal background will limit the number of words that have meaning for them. This vocabulary deficiency may be the result of lower-class socioeconomic backgrounds, bilingual family situations, or interests that preclude extensive use of verbal symbols. Although the problem is difficult, the school can do much to overcome such environmental influences by providing oral language experiences, instruction in the use of context clues, and experience in listening to standard English.

**Weakness in comprehension.**   In some cases, because of poor word-recognition or word-attack skills, pupils may not be able to pay sufficient attention to the thought of the reading material, and as a result, comprehension may suffer. There are also some who, because of difficulty in concentration or because of interfering problems, cannot seem to "listen to themselves" as they read. Remediation here depends on the cause of the loss of understanding. Possibly remedial work may include work in vocabulary; it may require help in study skills or study methods; or it may even involve some sort of therapy so that problems are released and attention can again be paid to the academic task.

**Slow reading rate.**   Poor readers are often slow readers. Slow reading can be expected if students are reading below the sixth-grade level. Problems in word recognition and meaning are generally the causes. Remediation in such cases consists of helping students to develop a greater sight vocabulary, providing practice in oral reading with the emphasis on phrasing, and eliminating such habits as finger pointing, excessive head movements, and vocalization. Teaching speeded reading to students reading below the sixth-grade level is a poor practice. It is more likely to develop skippers and skimmers than to develop good readers.

For more information on diagnosing and correcting reading problems, see:

Bond, Guy L., and Tinker, Miles A. *Reading Difficulties: Their Diagnosis and Correction.* 2nd ed. New York: Appleton-Century-Crofts, 1967. Chapter 4.

Gallant, Ruth. *Handbook in Corrective Reading: Basic Tasks.* Columbus, Ohio: Charles E. Merrill, 1970. Chapter 2.

Wilson, Robert M. *Diagnostic and Remedial Reading for Classroom and Clinic.* Columbus, Ohio: Charles E. Merrill, 1967. Chapter 1.

## GROUPING AND SPECIAL CLASSES

In the elementary schools of the United States, various forms of grouping within the classroom are common practice. These groups may be based on ability (reading, verbal capacity, arithmetic, etc.); on particular needs (phonic elements, structural elements, main idea comprehension, etc.); on oral skills (speaking vocabulary, skill in discussion, etc.); on interests (type of materials, story preferences, etc.); on friendships (social compatibility, similarity in background, etc.); on socioeconomic levels; or on control of dominant and shy individuals. They may take the form of large or small groups, tutorial or pair situations, research groupings, or the whole class may operate as one group.

The teacher who groups children in the classroom is not eliminating heterogeneity but rather controlling certain of its conditions so that instruction and learning are more effective and efficient.

### Principles of Grouping

Grouping is one (and only one) of the basic ways of providing for individual differences. But it can be a very effective way if certain principles are followed. A cardinal principle is that there is no one right or wrong way of grouping. The manner of grouping should contribute directly to solving specific administrative and teaching problems, and should be chosen to fit the situation. Flexibility is important here. Groups should change in composition and purpose as pupils learn and as situations and needs change.

Just as there is no one right way of grouping, so there is no standard or ideal number of groups per class or students per group. It is better to have two well-run, businesslike ability groups, for example, than to have four or five disorganized groups. And within the group, purpose should be the major determinant of size. In some cases, the whole class may be considered a group. In others, two persons are enough to be classified as a group. If discipline is a problem, small groups are best because they give pupils more of a chance to participate.

Determining who should be in which group is primarily a teacher's decision. Testing can be very helpful but thoughtful teacher judgment may prove better than test results, particularly in cases of students with special problems. Occasionally, however, students should take part in choosing some of their own groups. This is one way to capitalize on their motivations and understandings of one another.

Finally in setting up and using group procedures, two special cautions should be noted. First, care must be taken to make sure that value judgments about the groups and individuals within the groups are avoided. Names of groups should not imply status or ability in any way. Second, much attention should be paid ahead of time to the variety and pace of the groups' work. Planning will guarantee that each group is working toward its purposes at all times.

For a complete treatment of this subject, see:

Robinson, Helen M. *Reading Instruction in Various Patterns of Grouping.* Supplementary Educational Monograph, No. 89. Chicago: University of Chicago Press, 1959.

### Remedial Classes Versus the Regular Classroom

One of the temptations that many content teachers find difficult to resist is that of attempting to turn over all of the reading problems to a special remedial teacher. Of course, once one understands that all of those who read below grade level are not remediable, this solution does not seem quite as attractive. From 10 to 15 percent of the children in school can profit from remedial instruction; at least that many more are below the average group but doing as well as they are able. But the problem in the school is always where and how to handle the instruction.

The classroom teacher is the most important individual in any reading program, whether developmental, corrective, or remedial. However, with large class sizes, wide ranges of ability, and possibly inadequate instruction, it seems likely that reading problems are often *produced* in the regular classroom. Perfect teaching and a perfect teaching situation would mean very few remedial or corrective cases, but such perfection is not often found. Furthermore, if the number of *well-trained* teachers increases at a slower rate proportionately than the number of children, as is happening in many parts of the United States today, the proportion of reading disability cases is most likely to increase.

In view of this situation, it is safe to say that the regular classroom teacher is probably not able to handle the severe reading disability case. The child may have physical, emotional, or environmental handicaps which make him or her quite "exceptional" in terms of most of the children in the class. She, or more likely, he (the chances are at least five to one that it will be a boy) is so different from the rest of the group that the teacher may despair of ever being able to reach the child. This type of student is obviously in need of a special remedial situation.

Corrective instruction, where only certain skills are deficient, may be handled by the regular classroom teacher. Special emphases can be given within the group; special exercises may be found which the child can do independently and individually or in small groups; and a few minutes of individual "tutoring" may be provided occasionally. Because the problem is not pervasive but concerned with only smaller aspects of reading skill, it can be alleviated in small lessons which are possible for the regular teacher. Programmed and individualized materials are becoming increasingly available.

Of course the major efforts of any school district should be toward the improvement of developmental reading in every classroom since this will diminish the frequency of remedial or corrective cases. But conflict arises here. While almost everyone wants a remedial clinic or a special remedial class, the funds necessary to set up this remedial situation are usually taken from general school revenues resulting in larger class size throughout the school.

Remedial classes *are* expensive. A clinical approach is even more so, making it out of the reach of most districts because of the specialized personnel necessary. A remedial group must be small, must meet regularly, must have a teacher with special preparation, and must include special equipment and materials. The groups must be carefully formed after individual evaluation and testing to diagnose problems. Where such classes have been formed, however, they have usually been quite successful, and most of the regular classroom teachers have supported the idea.

The following points are reasonable considerations in the approach to the problem:

1.  A special remedial class can be very helpful if other educational goals do not suffer. If class size will not be increased by the addition of a remedial program, it will provide dividends in the form of parent and public relations, improved reading skill of problem cases, fewer behavior problems,

and some relief for the regular classroom teacher which cannot be achieved in any other way.

2.   Corrective reading should remain in the province of the regular classroom teacher. It is somewhat like educational "first aid" and may occur at any time during the school year whenever the need arises. Furthermore, although special preparation may be quite helpful, it is not absolutely necessary.

3.   A remedial group does not need to be segregated for the total school day. It is better if the child comes to the remedial teacher for an hour or less daily and then returns to the regular class for the rest of the day. In this way, the benefits of the special situation can be provided for more children, and the stigma of being in the "dummy class" is at least partially avoided.

4.   The regular teacher and the special reading teacher should maintain close contact at all times in regard to individual children. Planning must be continuous in both classes. This is a team job.

5.   If there is doubt among a majority of the faculty, if money is not readily obtainable without undermining other aspects of the program, or if a properly prepared teacher is not available, the remedial program should probably not be attempted. In that case, special efforts might be made to prepare all the faculty in remedial reading procedures that could be employed in the regular classroom.

There are other possible remedial arrangements which larger districts can undertake. See, for example, the San Diego plan in the article by Lee cited below. For other examples of remediation programs, see:

Carrillo, Lawrence. "Reactions For and Against the Special Remedial Reading Class," *California Journal of Secondary Education* 31 (December 1957), 450–54.

Kottmeyer, William. *Teacher's Guide for Remedial Reading.* Manchester, Mo.: Webster, 1959, pp. 240–52.

Lee, Dwight. "San Diego City Schools: Four Programs for Underachievers," *NEA Journal* (November 1962).

*The Reading Teacher* 15, 6 (May 1962), entire issue.

Strang, Ruth, and Bracken, Dorothy. *Making Better Readers.* Boston: D. C. Heath, 1957, pp. 289–338.

# 7 FACTORS ASSOCIATED WITH READING DIFFICULTY

No single consistent cause of failure in reading has ever been isolated. The problems which occur are usually a result of a number of factors operating in, on, and around the individual. Anyone who blames a lack of phonics in the reading program, or *any other single factor*, simply has not investigated the literature nor worked with many problem cases.

In order to discuss factors associated with reading difficulty, some categories must be used. This discussion isolates (1) physical, (2) intellectual, (3) psychological, (4) environmental, and (5) educational factors. Though each will be discussed separately, it is important to keep in mind that factors in reading difficulties commonly occur as interrelated constellations rather than as single, assignable causes.

## PHYSICAL FACTORS

The classroom teacher is in a good position to detect signs of physical difficulties and to initiate referrals to the specialist equipped to handle these problems. No teacher should attempt to diagnose or prescribe treatment for physical ailments but should refer any suspected cases to the school nurse and the doctor. Because correction of the disability may be possible and because such correction is likely to be reflected by improved academic work, the teacher's responsibility is to understand what may happen to a child with a physical problem, to refer him or her for corrective treatment, and to reteach material when the child is in better condition to learn.

The most common physical problems are those related to visual acuity, auditory perception, and general health. How teachers can determine the existence of such problems deserves further discussion.

### Visual Difficulties

Many persons have become good readers in spite of visual problems, but if poor vision is added to other difficulties, the combination of problems is likely to result in a reading disability. Research indicates that visual acuity as measured normally by the Snellen Chart has little to do with reading problems.

The Snellen Chart (American Optical Company; Southbridge, Mass.) will detect nearsightedness and should be used if more comprehensive tests are not available. (Farsightedness and astigmatism, however, are often more pertinent to reading difficulty, and visual acuity at reading distance should also be measured.) When the chart is used in the school, the student is placed twenty feet from the chart and asked to read the letters seen. Each eye is tested separately while the other eye is covered. A score of 20/20 is considered normal. This means that at twenty feet from the chart, the eye being tested can see what the normal eye sees at twenty feet. A score of 20/40 means that this eye can only see at twenty feet what the normal eye sees at forty feet. A score of 20/30 is considered borderline and represents an acuity only 8.5 percent less than 20/20.

Testing for visual acuity can also be done with the AMA Rating Reading Card (American Medical Association; 535 North Dearborn Street; Chicago).

There are other instruments that test many aspects of vision. For example, the Ortho-Rater (Bausch and Lomb Optical Company; Rochester, N.Y.) tests acuity, binocular coordination, fusion at near- and far-point, depth perception, and color vision. A school model is available. It can be operated by a teacher or nurse with little training necessary, and it will test large numbers of pupils rather rapidly. The *Keystone Visual Survey Tests* (Keystone View Company; Meadville, Pa.), employing an instrument called the Telebinocular, show acuity, muscle balance, fusion, depth, and color perception, and are easily administered. The *Eames Eye Tests* (Harcourt Brace Jovanovich; New York) screen for acuity, nearsightedness and farsightedness, muscular balance, fusion, and astigmatism.

Some of these tests tend to overrefer, that is, they will seem to locate a few more problems than actually exist or need correction. However, when combined with teacher observations they ordinarily provide an adequate basis for referral. The teacher might watch for the following signs of visual defects:

Inability to distinguish between words that look alike

Difficulty in reading either from the board or from the book, or both

A tendency to hold the book in strange positions, to keep it very close to the eyes or at arm's length

Facial contortions such as frowning, scowling, or squinting

A tendency to rub the eyes frequently, or to complain of dizziness, headaches, or nausea after close work

Red-rimmed eyelids, scales or crusts on the eyelids, frequent sties, or continual watering of the eyes

A difference in the size of the pupils of the two eyes, or greatly dilated pupils

One eye that deviates from the other in direction, either vertically or
    horizontally

Extreme sensitivity to light, or shutting or covering one eye

A tendency to tilt the head or thrust it forward when attempting to focus
    the eyes

Many other references on visual difficulties are available. See, for
example:

Austin, Mary C., Bush, Clifford L., and Huebner, Mildred H. *Reading Evaluation.* New York: The Ronald Press, 1961, pp. 52–59.

Bond, Guy L., and Tinker, Miles A. *Reading Difficulties: Their Diagnosis and Correction.* 2nd ed. New York: Appleton-Century-Crofts, 1967, pp. 102–09.

Kennedy, Eddie C. *Classroom Approaches to Remedial Reading.* Itasca, Ill.: F. E. Peacock, 1971, pp. 394–98.

Spache, George D. *Toward Better Reading.* Champaign, Ill.: Garrard, 1963, pp. 103–08.

### Hearing Loss

Hearing impairment may be an important factor contributing to reading
disability, especially if the loss is severe or if there is high-frequency deafness. The beginning stages of reading are based primarily on language that
has been heard. Some teaching methods are founded on auditory discrimination (especially phonics and oral reading), and some aspects of these methods
are included in almost any method of teaching reading.

Studies have indicated that about 3 to 20 percent of the schoolchildren
tested had hearing deficiencies. At least 5 percent of these children had
hearing losses that could interfere with learning.

Two aspects of auditory sensation that can be tested are loudness, measured as hearing acuity in sound-pressure units called decibels, and pitch,
measured as tone frequency in cycles per second. A loss of ten decibels or
more should be used as a practical standard for referral to a specialist. A
hearing loss of over twenty decibels is almost certain to handicap the pupil.
High-tone deafness should always be checked since acute hearing in the high
frequency ranges is needed for hearing some of the consonant sounds.

For purpose of identifying pupils who need careful medical examination
of hearing, the school may use an audiometer. Currently available types are
the (1) Audio Development Company (ADC) Audiometer (Audiometer
Sales Corporation; Minneapolis, Minn.); (2) Maico Audiometer (Maico
Electronics, Inc.; Minneapolis, Minn.); (3) Sonotone Pure-Tone Audiometer (Sonotone Corporation; Elmsford, N.Y.); and (4) Western Electric
Company Audiometer (Graybar Electric Company; New York).

Each company has several models, including portable and clinical types. Some will test up to forty pupils at one time and others are for use with individuals. Prices range from under $300 to over $1000.

Less formal tests such as the whisper test, the watch-tick test, and a talking test are discussed by Jack Kough and Robert DeHaan.[1] These tests are not nearly so accurate as the audiometer but can be used for screening. If a hearing difficulty is present, the teacher is likely to note the following symptoms:

—Difficulty in or impossibility of learning phonics

—Tendency to avoid oral reading (since speech problems are often related to hearing loss)

—A dislike for group work, especially discussion (since hearing difficulty makes participation more difficult)

—Unnatural voice pitch or strength

—Indistinct or faulty speech, especially where certain sounds are consistently omitted

—Frequent failure to respond to questions, or frequent requests for repetition

—Tendency to strain forward or frown when listening or a tendency to turn one ear toward the speaker

—A seeming inability to determine the direction from which sounds come when the pupil is a member of the group

—Discharge from the ear, earaches, and complaints of a ringing or constant noise in the ears

—Frequent colds or sinus infections

For more on hearing impediments, see:

Austin, Mary C., Bush, Clifford L., and Huebner, Mildred H. *Reading Evaluation.* New York: The Ronald Press, 1961, pp. 59–64.

Schubert, Delwyn G., and Torgerson, Theodore L. *Improving the Reading Program.* 3rd ed. Dubuque, Iowa: William C. Brown, 1972, pp. 42–43.

Smith, Henry P., and Dechant, Emerald V. *Psychology in Teaching Reading.* Englewood Cliffs, N.J.: Prentice-Hall, 1961, pp. 135–40.

Spache, George D. *Toward Better Reading.* Champaign, Ill.: Garrard, 1963, pp. 113–14.

Strang, Ruth. *Diagnostic Teaching of Reading.* New York: McGraw-Hill, 1964, pp. 181–83.

### General Health

Children who do not feel well cannot be expected to do well in their classes. Teachers should be alert for:

---

[1] *Identifying Children with Special Needs*, Vol. 1, elem. ed. (Chicago: Science Research Associates, 1955), 78–80.

Extended or repeated absences from school

Rapid exhaustion, lethargy, or listlessness

Marked underweight or overweight conditions

Excessive restlessness or overactivity

Fainting

Pains in arms, legs, or joints

Low-grade fevers or frequent colds

Certain chronic conditions may lower a pupil's vitality. Rheumatic fever, asthma, malnutrition, and thyroid deficiency are the most common ailments associated with reading difficulties. Fatigue can also make it difficult for the child to become interested in or to enjoy reading. His or her attention will suffer and comprehension will drop. Insufficient sleep may be a problem common to poor readers since it lowers the amount of energy available for classroom work. Cumulative records should be studied for evidence of health problems, and space should be provided on the records for teachers' notations.

When lengthy absences from school have occurred, one of the best indications of the grade level of the remedial work needed is the child's grade placement at the time of the absences. Teachers should talk with the school nurse or doctor to learn more about any specific health problem noted in the records and should attempt to adapt classroom conditions to suit the situation. Where physical problems exist, the responsibility of the school is primarily to refer the student to a competent agency upon discovery of the difficulty, but also to follow up at frequent intervals and determine what can be done to encourage progress in learning.

For further reference, see:

Carter, Homer L. J., and McGinnis, Dorothy J. *Diagnosis and Treatment of the Disabled Reader.* New York: Macmillan, 1970, pp. 52–53, 299–300.

Smith, Henry P., and Dechant, Emerald V. *Psychology in Teaching Reading.* Englewood Cliffs, N.J.: Prentice-Hall, 1961, pp. 154–82.

Wilson, Robert M. *Diagnostic and Remedial Reading: For Classroom and Clinic.* Columbus, Ohio: Charles E. Merrill, 1967, pp. 41–42.

## INTELLECTUAL FACTORS

The discussion in the first chapter of this book has already referred to the relation between intelligence and reading. To repeat, the potential for reading achievement is in large part determined by the intelligence of the individual. Therefore, in spite of their weaknesses, intelligence tests are an indispensable tool in reading diagnosis. But tests which require reading to obtain answers should not be used with poor readers. Group pencil-and-paper tests will be sufficiently accurate for average and above-average readers.

The issue of whether heredity or environment determines intelligence is a false one. A number of studies have shown that by creating a stimulating environment a child's measured intelligence can be raised up to twenty points or even more within a period of six months to several years. The conclusion seems warranted that many children, given the proper environment, can definitely improve their "potential."

For further information on this factor, see:

Ekwell, Eldon E. *Psychological Factors in the Teaching of Reading.* Columbus, Ohio: Charles E. Merrill, 1973. Chapter 6.

Guszak, Frank J. *Diagnostic Reading Instruction in the Elementary School.* New York: Harper & Row, 1972. Chapter 10.

## PERSONAL-PSYCHOLOGICAL FACTORS

In at least 50 percent of reading disability cases, there are emotional concomitants. In many cases the emotional difficulty takes precedence, and unless it is at least partially solved, little progress can be made. On the other hand, there is likely to be a circular effect where the reading difficulty causes the emotional problem and it in turn increases the reading difficulty. In a complete program for the improvement of reading, personality factors should be appraised.

When the appraisal shows that an emotional problem exists, teachers should try to determine whether it is the reading or the emotional problem that is primarily at fault. If it is lack of achievement in reading, teaching can be geared to the problem to relieve the emotional tensions. The pupil may then make a better adjustment in other aspects of his or her development.

If the emotional problem is primary, teaching, no matter how skilled, will probably not succeed. A pupil with a serious problem *from his or her point of view* will be most concerned with that problem and must come to a satisfactory solution before achieving anything in the academic area. Also, such serious emotional cases should not be included in a remedial reading program. The program will only suffer, and the child's problem will certainly not be solved.

If the school employs a psychologist or guidance counselor skilled in the use of psychological testing instruments, that person should be given free rein in choosing and using those instruments. Testing and providing therapy for children with emotional difficulties takes a great deal of time. Most schools do not attempt therapy, but they may note symptoms and refer cases to therapists in private practice or in public clinics. These people are better equipped to handle the more serious problems than are the schools.

In the elementary school such instruments and procedures as checklists of traits, sociometric techniques, observational and anecdotal records, autobiographies, individual conferences, projective techniques, or personality inventories may be used, although certain of these tools should be used only by qualified persons. If a psychometrist or psychologist is doing the investigation, he or she will employ the tests most familiar to him or her. If anyone else is to do the testing, a psychologist should be consulted before any test materials are purchased.

If the school has no faculty member with specific training in this area, general survey tests of personality could be investigated and *perhaps* employed. Be sure, however, that no attempt is made to diagnose cases or to do therapy based on the results of these tests. *Use them only to screen for the remedial program and to refer cases to competent persons.*

### Psychological Tests

The following annotated list may be helpful for determining whether remediation or referral is necessary:

*Behavior Preference Record.* Monterey, Calif.: California Test Bureau. Grades 4–6, 7–9 (30–45 minutes). Gives a series of problem situations followed by three to five possible courses of action and reasons for choosing them. Yields scores for cooperation, friendliness, integrity, leadership, responsibility, and level of critical thinking.

*California Test of Personality.* Monterey, Calif.: California Test Bureau. Grades 4–8, 7–10 (about 50 minutes). Scores on self-adjustment and social adjustment, combined from several smaller subareas.

*Mental Health Analysis.* Monterey, Calif.: California Test Bureau. Grades 4–8, 7–9 (45–50 minutes). Contains two general sections, "Mental Health Assets" and "Mental Health Liabilities," each section based on five components.

*Mooney Problem Check List.* New York: The Psychological Corporation. Grades 7–9 (35–50 minutes). Scores attitudes about health and physical development, school, home and family, money, work and the future, boy and girl relationships, relationships to people, and self-centeredness.

*Personal and Social Development Program.* Chicago: Science Research Associates. Grades 4–8. Provides for recording trends in the individual's personal and social behavior. Includes an extensive teacher's guide to help in interpretation and guidance.

*SRA Junior Inventory.* Chicago: Science Research Associates. Grades 4–8 (about 40 minutes). Gives problem checklists for the areas of school, home, self, other people, and things in general.

### Bibliotherapy

Reading may occasionally be utilized as an approach to emotional adjustment. Reading materials carefully selected to meet the needs of the individual can have a therapeutic effect. In fact, such reading is usually referred to as "bibliotherapy" (see the discussions in Shrodes and Smith and Dechant listed below).

Books may be used that offer help to children in overcoming an emotional difficulty. By evaluating their own experiences through reliving them with the characters in a story or by gaining an insight into the problems of others, they may accept themselves and their own problems more easily. Great or rapid help for an individual is not to be expected from this approach, yet it is a type of therapy available for use by the classroom teacher.

For further information on emotional problems and reading, see:

Austin, Mary C., Bush, Clifford L., and Huebner, Mildred H. *Reading Evaluation.* New York: The Ronald Press, 1961, pp. 71–78.

Bond, Guy L., and Tinker, Miles A. *Reading Difficulties: Their Diagnosis and Correction.* 2nd ed. New York: Appleton-Century-Crofts, 1967, pp. 128–34.

Ekwall, Eldon E. *Psychological Factors in the Teaching of Reading.* Columbus, Ohio: Charles E. Merrill, 1973. Chapter 5.

Fry, Edward. *Reading Instruction for Classroom and Clinic.* New York: McGraw-Hill, 1972. Chapter 17.

Shrodes, Caroline. "Bibliotherapy." *The Reading Teacher* (October 1955), pp. 24–29.

Smith, H. P., and Dechant, E. V. *Psychology in Teaching Reading.* Englewood Cliffs, N.J.: Prentice-Hall, 1961. (See especially pp. 316–20 for a list of books for bibliotherapy classified by problem areas.)

## ENVIRONMENTAL FACTORS

Of the innumerable environmental forces playing upon children, the most influential forces appear in the social groupings of the home, family, friends, and associates.

The verbal development of children may indicate the verbal environment that they have experienced. If a language other than English is spoken in the home, it is little wonder that children raised in this environment have difficulty in reading English in print. They have heard hardly any words of this type before entering school, and they may not have used many of the English words found in beginning books.

It is also true that reading is not a cherished skill in every home and with every family. If children never see their parents read, they can only assume that this is not a very useful skill. It will appear that only teachers feel reading is important.

Often the problems of children seem to be a result of tensions in the home. Tensions which develop in the home are carried to the school, and are likely to interfere with learning. The opposite is also true—tensions that develop in the school setting are carried home.

Irregular school attendance and frequent changing of schools may result from the transiency of a family. An inactive, extremely homey, or solitary life may cause problems in children's acquisition of enough experience for the reading process. In other words, the experiences children have in the family and in a neighborhood setting are reflected in their school behavior and in their ability to learn in school.

The writer has participated in two studies of the relation between environmental differences and reading problems.[2] These studies concluded that:

1. Home environment is important in the genesis of reading ability, especially as it related to parental attitudes of personal enjoyment in reading, acceptance of the school, and pride in children's accomplishments. The presence of other children of the same age in the neighborhood also seems important.

2. The records of the prenatal period and birth offer important data inasmuch as poor readers tend to have a history of (a) delivery before full term, (b) smaller size at birth, and (c) injury at birth.

3. In developing, retarded readers seem to share a background of (a) slower development of verbal skills, (b) a higher likelihood of speech defects, (c) slowness in toilet training and a tendency toward enuresis, and (d) slower motor development.

4. The emotional histories of poor readers indicate a lack of (a) adjustment to change, (b) friends, and (c) independence.

Note that even in these conclusions, environment, physical development, and emotions become intermixed. This illustrates the complex causation of reading disability and the impossibility of assigning single factors as causes.

Very often there is little that can be done by the school to change environmental factors inhibiting pupil progress. However, better understanding may sometimes be achieved by the teachers, and this at least may help children to adjust to that portion of their lives spent in school. Occasionally that is enough to help overcome serious environmental problems.

To understand the environmental factors influencing students, teachers can use personal data blanks and student autobiographies. Taking a study tour of the community in which students live may also help. The most personal approach is to visit homes and arrange parent-teacher conferences. Many parents of poor readers in remedial classes or those who find their child included in the low group will be happy to have a conference with the teacher and will welcome a chance to help overcome their child's problem. Such things as changing the reading atmosphere of the home can have a real effect on children's approach to reading in school.

[2] W. D. Sheldon and L. W. Carrillo, "Relation of Parents, Home, and Certain Developmental Characteristics to Children's Reading Ability," *Elementary School Journal* (January 1952), pp. 262–70; and L. W. Carrillo "The Relation of Certain Environmental and Developmental Factors to Reading Ability in Children" (Ph.D. diss., Syracuse University, 1957).

For more references on environmental influences, see also:

Ekwall, Eldon E. *Psychological Factors in the Teaching of Reading.* Columbus, Ohio: Charles E. Merrill, 1973. Chapters 9 and 13.

Froehlich, Clifford, and Hoyt, Kenneth. *Guidance Testing.* Chicago: Science Research Associates, 1959. Chapters 14, 15, and 16.

Wilson, Robert M., and Hall, Maryanne. *Reading and the Elementary School Child.* New York: Van Nostrand Reinhold, 1972. Chapter 15.

## EDUCATIONAL FACTORS

Some factors within the school situation may also lead to reading difficulty. For purposes of discussion, they may be broadly classified as shortcomings in administration, in planning and methods, and in communication both outside and inside the classroom.

### Administrative Problems

Administrative problems affect large numbers of students. One obvious problem that may result in reading disability is overly large classes. In any classroom of more than thirty, there is a tendency to neglect children at both ends of the achievement scale. Twenty-five pupils is more nearly the optimum class.

Besides class size, another large-scale failure of the system is in the lack of qualified personnel. The lack may result from the unavailability of certain teachers (in the area of special diagnosis and service, for example). Or there may simply be many teachers in the system poorly prepared for the teaching of reading, having had no recent college courses in reading methods.

Even when there are many qualified teachers in the system, the administration may fail by taking planning time away from creative teachers and imposing clerical, public relations, or other duties. Some of this may be necessary, but too much almost always stops the teaching process.

### Problems in Planning Materials and Methods

Aside from the administrative aspects of the system, there are specific teaching practices that may result in reading problems. Using curricular materials that lack variety or range is a common failing. Materials of varying interest are needed so that all children can find something they really want in their reading. Similarly, a wide range of material is needed so that average students are not given reading beyond their skills and bright children are not limited to the level of their on-grade readers.

Even if there is a sufficiently broad range of reading material available, reading difficulties may result if students are not systematically exposed to it. One common error is to emphasize covering material rather than learning a skill. Another is to expect too much too soon from children, an error fostered by parents and teachers alike. Reading lessons must be properly structured.

Failure to develop interest and readiness for the lesson almost always leads to problems later. So does neglecting to follow through by carefully introducing new words and their meaning and testing comprehension in all areas, not just the recall of directly stated facts. These problems in method, of course, are related to the above-mentioned problem of poorly prepared teachers.

### Communication Problems

Teachers are primarily communicators. They exchange information almost constantly within the classroom, but they also have to exercise this function with the outside world. Reading problems are sometimes compounded by poor exchange of information about problem cases between teachers, administrators, and parents. Clashes between parents and teachers about a child's progress can be detrimental since home reinforcement is essential for reading development. Breakdowns in communication between teachers can lead to uncoordinated and discontinuous reading instruction through the first eight grades.

Communication within the classroom can also be problematic. A very troublesome source of classroom misunderstanding arises from the fact that while most primary teachers are women, most problem readers are boys. Some reasons why boys encounter more difficulties are inherent in the school situation. Girls tend to excel in the verbal areas, and most school tasks are verbal. Boys and girls mature at different rates, though both are admitted at the same chronological age. The school environment, materials, and curriculum seem to be more frustrating to boys than to girls. Finally, pressure is often exerted on boys to do well even when they actually cannot.

Because differences in point of view exist between the sexes, the predominance of women teachers in the early grades may increase the risk of boys' being misunderstood. It is imperative, therefore, that the classroom teacher make special efforts to understand the boys in her room. She can anticipate that some of them will have much more trouble in learning than others, and she should be alert for the first signs of difficulty. In the intermediate and upper grades, it is likely that curricular provisions such as working groups based on special interests may be necessary.

For more information on how the educational system contributes to reading difficulties, see:

Barbe, Walter B. "Instructional Causes of Poor Reading," in Leo M. Schell, and Paul C. Burns, eds., *Remedial Reading.* Boston: Allyn & Bacon, 1968.

Greene, Frank P., ed. *Reading: Reasons and Readiness.* Syracuse, N.Y.: School of Education, Syracuse University, 1970.

Heilman, Arthur W. *Principles and Practices of Teaching Reading.* Columbus, Ohio: Charles E. Merrill, 1967. Chapter 13.

# 8 CHARACTERISTICS OF A SOUND REMEDIAL PROGRAM

A good remedial program is not much different from a good developmental program. The major difference seems to be that the children are older and not at the grade level at which they should be reading. There are, however, considerations and characteristics of remedial programs that should be investigated.

## ADMINISTRATIVE CONSIDERATIONS

Because a special remedial program is comparatively expensive, it deserves to be well planned with the cooperation of all concerned. Teachers must be selected carefully.

The groups should be small. If a special group is to be started with a specialized teacher, preference should be given to those students with reading abilities far below their potential.

Major remedial efforts should be made at the fourth-grade and the eighth-grade level. But level of grade attainment should be disregarded when forming special groups. It is more desirable for all children in the group to be at approximately the same level in reading or to have the same types of problems, regardless of grade placement.

The groups should meet at regular intervals. If possible, meetings should be daily, lasting for at least thirty minutes but not more than one hour.

Status of the remedial class is important, too. If he or she is not too busy, the principal of a school might help out as much as possible. One of the best classes this writer has seen was taught by the vice-principal.

## CHARACTERISTICS OF GOOD REMEDIAL TEACHERS

Good remedial teachers share certain personal characteristics. First and foremost, they genuinely like children. Their sensitivity to the emotional needs of children in their charge is conveyed by their warmth, tact, and sympathetic understanding. They are also generally optimists who can tolerate some failure. Preordained goals that must be reached are not as important to them as steady progress at the individual child's own pace.

Aside from these more or less innate qualities, there are two other characteristics that good remedial teachers have acquired. Knowledge—of the reading program through the grades, of remedial methods and materials, and of the referral agencies in the community—is acquired with training and constant reading in the field. The ability to communicate with parents, other teachers, and administrators and to get them interested in the program is developed over long years of experience.

## PRINCIPLES OF REMEDIAL TEACHING

The successful teaching of remedial reading requires that the teacher first attempt to find out what is wrong. The initial diagnosis should determine what the level of instruction for the poor reader should be so that material at the reading and interest level of the student can be assigned. After this diagnosis, a concentrated effort to improve areas of difficulty can be made. Diagnosis and evaluation of progress will continue throughout the program.

Maintaining the interest of the poor reader in the program is very important. Part of this objective can be achieved by creating a positive atmosphere. The poor reader must be helped to feel that he or she is liked, appreciated, and understood. Successful experiences are essential, especially in the early stages, to overcome the negative after-effects of frustration and failure. Another important way of maintaining interest is to keep the learner involved in the analysis of his or her problem, in the plans for solving it, and in the evaluation of progress. With respect to evaluation, the units of improvement should be small enough so that progress can be recorded at frequent intervals. Every sign of improvement in work should be noted and called to the child's attention. Also, that pupil's progress should be compared only with his or her *own* past performance.

This emphasis on keeping the program pupil-centered does not mean that it should be loosely structured. On the contrary, a remedial situation should have a careful structure of planned activities. The child may choose things to do but only within a framework limited to those activities that will help him or her. Reasonable limits of behavior must be firmly set. Parents are perhaps most able to help at this planning stage, since they are usually not as effective with direct teaching.

Careful records should be kept in an individual folder for each child. Excessive testing should be avoided, however, even at the beginning of the program.

Finally, remedial reading specialists should perhaps heed one caution. Any teacher who specializes has a tendency to adopt the "specialist complex." It is too easy to feel that the field to which one is devoting a total effort is the most important and that other areas of the curriculum pale by comparison. Reading training is important to a child's development, but it is certainly only a part of it.


## REMEDIATION AND THE PARENT

Help at home for the retarded reader can be a two-edged sword. Many children with reading disabilities have already experienced a great deal of help at home from parents or siblings. Parents are often unskilled at teaching, and their ideas of what should be taught may be at variance with the views of the school. This confuses the child. Moreover, if the child is a poor reader, most parents who attempt to help become emotionally involved. For this reason they cannot teach effectively and the situation becomes tense. Negative feelings may be carried over to the school reading situation, resulting perhaps in a loss of skill rather than a gain. In cases where the reading problem has become severe, there is an appearance of stupidity that is difficult to overcome in the parent-child teaching situation.

All administrators recall unhappy sessions with parents of poor readers, and most teachers have had this same experience. These parents wholeheartedly wish to help their children. They realize that the boy or girl who cannot read well will not be able to succeed in our society. They want to do something—anything—that will help.

What can they be told? Many of these parents feel that the schools discourage them from giving their child any kind of help, and so they are likely to become bitter about what the school is doing. It is undoubtedly better to indicate some of the things that they *can* do but to keep the direction of such a program in the hands of the school.

Specific materials for teaching should be provided by the schools for use during home lessons. For example, a regular basal reader may be employed occasionally. If it is, the school should not give the child the same book that is being used in the classroom since the child tends to memorize the next day's lesson rather than to genuinely improve reading skills. The parent should have the teacher's edition to the basal reader used and should be encouraged to follow the lesson plan that is given for the teacher. This, of course, means a great deal of work, and the average parent may not take this much time. It is quite important that the parent follow the usual methods, however, because departures often mean that the pupil uses one learning method against the other and is likely not to learn either in school or at home.

Workbooks emphasizing phonics are usually dangerous to send home because adult readers may have evolved their own phonetic generalizations but be unable to teach them. The admonition "Sound it out" is of no help in phonetic word attack to a pupil who has a limited phonics background or who has had experience with only a limited variety of words.

Occasionally parents will buy children's editions of the basal reader being used in school, not realizing that reading is not taught as a content area. They believe that if the child memorizes the book, he or she has learned to read. Upon discovery of this situation, a teacher should contact the parents immediately and explain that the story in the reader is only a vehicle to teach the various skills rather than something to be learned as content.

Books and various kinds of games are sold for home use in teaching reading. In general, these workbooks, games, and kits may be criticized as covering only a small portion of the skill of learning to read. They tend to be isolated practice materials without particular overall organization. These are much more likely to help the child who is already progressing rapidly in reading, rather than the child who needs help.

### Books for Parents

If parents are willing to take the time to investigate reading programs more fully, the following sources are worthwhile:

Artley, A. S. *Your Child Learns to Read.* Chicago: Scott, Foresman, 1953.

Frank, Lawrence K., and Frank, Mary. *How to Help Your Child in School.* New York: The Viking Press, 1950.

Gates, Doris. *Helping Children Discover Books.* Chicago: Science Research Associates, 1956.

Goldenson, Robert. *Helping Your Child to Read Better.* New York: Thomas Y. Crowell, 1957.

*Janie Learns to Read.* Washington, D.C.: National Education Association, 1956.

Larrick, Nancy. *A Parent's Guide to Children's Reading.* New York: Doubleday, 1958. (Also Cardinal Edition. New York: Pocket Books, 1958.)

Rauch, Sidney J. *Handbook for the Volunteer Tutor.* Newark, Del.: International Reading Association, 1969.

Robison, Eleanor G. "A Letter to Parents." Contributions in Reading, No. 8. Boston: Ginn, 1958. (free leaflet)

Smith, Carl B., ed. *Parents and Reading: Perspectives in Reading.* No. 14. Newark, Del.: International Reading Association, 1971.

Strang, Ruth. *Helping Your Child Improve His Reading.* New York: E. P. Dutton, 1962.

Winebrenner, Rosemary. *How Can I Get My Teenager to Read?* Newark, Del.: International Reading Association, 1971.

In addition to the above references, professional sources include:

Bamman, Henry A., Dawson, Mildred A., and McGovern, James J. *Fundamentals of Basic Reading Instruction.* 3rd ed. New York: David McKay, 1973. Chapter 17.

Dallmann, Martha, et al. *The Teaching of Reading.* 4th ed. New York: Holt, Rinehart & Winston, 1974, pp. 525–39.

Department of Elementary School Principals. *Parents and the Schools.* Thirty-sixth Yearbook of the National Education Association. Washington, D.C.: National Education Association, 1957.

Freshour, Frank W. "Beginning Reading: Parents Can Help." *The Reading Teacher* 24 (January 1971), 511–16.

Grant, Eva H. *Parents and Teachers as Partners.* Chicago: Science Research Associates, 1952.

Hymes, James L. *Effective Home-School Relations.* Englewood Cliffs, N.J.: Prentice-Hall, 1953.

Langdon, Grace, and Stout, Irving W. *Helping Parents Understand Their Child's School.* Englewood Cliffs, N.J.: Prentice-Hall, 1957.

Wallen, Carl J., and Sebesta, Sam Leaton. *Readings on Teaching Reading.* Chicago: Science Research Associates, 1972, pp. 284–88.

### *Parent-Teacher Meetings*

Parents often appreciate meetings or programs designed to give more information about the school's reading program. A back-to-school night, an open house, or a visiting day may provide beginning orientation. These short meetings do not ordinarily provide a great deal of specific information, but they may help by showing a basic reading lesson, by discussing what is to be included in the program, or by providing a situation that initiates conferences between parents and teachers. Book fairs and exhibits may also help by showing new books that are of interest to children.

A series of discussion groups or PTA meetings can be set up to give more complete information regarding the school reading program. Topics could be selected by the parents from a list of questions such as:

What causes a reading difficulty?

What methods of teaching are used in the schools?

What provisions are made in the classroom for good readers and for poor readers?

How well are schools doing in the teaching of reading?

What can a parent do to help children in reading?

Is phonics the answer?

Are library books important?

How should we select books for a home library?

What happens in the reading program as the child moves up through the grades?

Should parents, as a group, help the schools in the purchase of books, films, and visual aids?

### Some Practical Suggestions for Parents

Other than actual tutoring, there are many things that can and should be done in the home by the family rather than in the school. In this area, teachers may suggest but not demand. As teachers, we should realize that a wider range of differences exists between homes than between schools and that a few of our suggestions will therefore be automatically rejected in some homes and families.

Presented below is a portion of a brochure adapted from *Help Your Child to Succeed in Reading* (Sonoma County, Calif.). While acting as a county reading supervisor, the writer used it in meetings with parents. The ideas can be used to promote better reading programs, to show some types of causation, to stress the fact that there can be many causes of poor reading, and to give suggestions for topics that might be discussed in a meeting.

For other practical suggestions for parents, see:

Schubert, Delwyn G., and Torgerson, Theodore L. *Improving the Reading Program*. Dubuque, Iowa: William C. Brown, 1972. Appendix D, "Letter to Parents of Disabled Readers."

## WHAT HELPS TO ENSURE SUCCESS IN READING?

**Good physical health**
> Proper diet
> Adequate rest
> Good vision and hearing
> Sufficient energy

**Good mental health**
> Vocabulary based on broad experiences
> A need to learn and an eagerness to try
> Freedom from severe emotional strain
> A feeling of acceptance by others—belonging
> A feeling of self-worth
> Ability to follow directions
> Ability to pay attention for a reasonable period of time

**Good home environment**
> Home values that include a sense of the importance of education
> A settled and congenial home
> Reading as an essential part of living in the home

Simple responsibilities
Conversations between child and parent

## Good educational situation
Uncrowded classrooms
Qualified teachers
Varied materials
Acceptance of the pupil at his own level of development
Adequate school plant

Take a careful look at the list. It is obvious that learning to read does not occur only in the school. Many factors of major concern in the home, and not the school, affect the ability to read. This is the reason that schools enlist the aid of the parents in the teaching of reading. A part of the job belongs to the school and a part belongs to the parents.

## YOU CAN HELP

Here is a list of things to do. Notice how these suggestions are tied in with the factors associated with reading success in the previous list. You are probably already doing many of these things. (Did you know you were teaching reading?) It is also probable that in your situation you cannot follow all the suggestions. It is not necessary to follow them all—any will help, and these are merely suggestions.

### *Physical*

1.   As nearly as possible, set regular hours for rest and sleep, especially on school nights. If homework interferes with regular sleep, let the school know.

2.   Arrange for an unhurried breakfast. Try to see that meals supply all of the nutrients needed for proper growth and well-being.

3.   If there are any indications of difficulty in hearing or seeing, arrange for an examination of the child.

4.   If your child appears to be ill, protect both him and the other children by keeping him home.

5.   Your child's general health should be checked regularly by the family physician.

### *Mental and Emotional*

1.   Read stories to your child. Be sure they are stories that he appreciates hearing.

2. Start a library that belongs to the child—have shelf space just for his books. If you read any of the books, discuss them with him but remember that his opinion is as important to him as yours is to you.

3. Whenever you do things together, talk about them together. Let the child express himself even if some of the ideas are not completely correct.

4. Show your boy or girl how written directions are used in the things you must do such as setting up materials or following recipes.

5. Help your child feel that he is an important member of the family. Include him in everything possible, even though it may take a little longer to do the job. Value his contributions no matter how small.

6. Answer his questions as well as you can but in simple terms. Don't try to give a complete answer all at once. Wait for the next question—you may be telling him more than he wants to know.

7. Give him an opportunity to work and play with other children near his age.

8. Accept, as parents, the fact of individual differences. Some people are verbal; others are not. Reading does not come easily and naturally to every child.

9. Have a time set aside for the sharing of reading by various members of the family. In this family reading circle, each member should have an opportunity to read his selection aloud to the others and discuss it if he wishes.

### *Home Environment*

1. If you find it necessary to move, remember that your boy or girl will try to make friends, to adjust to the new neighborhood, and to do almost everything else before he will proceed with his learning in reading.

2. Provide a time and place for reading. Although absolute quiet is not essential, the young reader should experience a minimum of distraction. Concentration for reading is difficult if the television or radio is never turned off and he cannot move away from the sound.

3. Set a good example for the child by showing how much you enjoy reading and how you profit from it. How often do *you* use your encyclopedia or dictionary?

4. Have a shelf of books that can be used by even the youngest child—books that can be torn by accident without creating bad feelings.

5. Try not to compare your child with others. He is different from everyone else and cannot be compared with anyone else.

6. Give your child simple things to do for which he alone is responsible. Show how much you appreciate it when he assumes responsibility.

7. Encourage your child by showing an interest in what is happening in school, but don't expect an answer to, "Well, what did you learn today?" Even an adult is unable to answer this question.

### *Education*

1. By your vote and your cooperation, help your community to provide better schools with sufficient money to secure additional space if needed, more materials, and teachers who are better prepared. It takes more dollars now than ever before to maintain schools.

2. Your children will reflect your expression of respect and friendliness for the school staff.

3. Do not expect teachers to be able to discipline an entire class better than you can discipline your own family. Attitudes learned at home are expressed in the school.

4. Visit the school and the classroom. Talk things over with the teacher.

5. If, after consulting your child's teacher, you decide to teach reading at home, make sure that you use the same system as the teacher but not the same books. Using a different system produces confusion; using the same books promotes memorization rather than reading.

---

## INTERESTING BOOKS FOR SLOWER READERS

Extensively annotated and graded book lists are available from a number of sources. For example:

*A Graded List of Books for School Libraries.* New York: Harcourt Brace Jovanovich. Contains a section on books for slow learners; revised often.

Harris, Albert J. *How to Increase Reading Ability.* New York: David McKay, 1961. Shows a complete list by grades and indicates those which have a much higher interest level than vocabulary level.

Spache, George D. *Good Reading for Poor Readers.* Champaign, Ill.: Garrard, 1972. Provides extensive listings by interest and vocabulary levels; well annotated and revised approximately every two years.

———. *Sources of Good Books for Poor Readers.* Newark, Del.: International Reading Association, 1969. Gives a listing of available reading lists.

Usually what the remedial teacher really wants is a series of books at least partially graded in difficulty and with interest levels higher than vocabulary levels. Many of these are now available, and a few are included in the list at the end of this section. Some of the series, however, contain a number of titles at approximately the same level rather than books that move upward in difficulty. The annotation of each item listed clarifies the type of series and gives the general theme.

Schools may wish to consult this list for ideas on adoption possibilities. However, before purchasing large quantities, they should send for copies of the books for examination and trial. They should also remember that in many cases there are no teachers' guides for these books, and hardly any of them provide any systematic procedure for the development of all the reading skills.

### Difficulty Levels Third Grade and Below

*American Indian Series.* Chandler, Edna Walker. Chicago: Benefic Press. Second- and third-grade difficulty. Dramatic stories of Indians, with picture dictionary of Indian words and teacher's notes.

*Aviation Readers.* Lent, Henry B., et al. New York: Macmillan. First-reader level to sixth. Interesting style, but those above second are factually dated.

*Basic Vocabulary Series.* Dolch, E. W., and Dolch, M. P. Champaign, Ill.: Garrard. High second grade in difficulty. Folk, animal, Indian stories based on Dolch Basic Sight Vocabulary and Commonest Nouns. Not very interesting above fourth grade.

*Beginner Books.* Dr. Seuss, et al. New York: Random House. High first- and second-grade difficulty. Large picture books with brief text (some in rhyme) about trains, fire engines, trucks, and so forth. Not too interesting above fifth grade.

*Books to Stretch On.* Hymes, James L., and O'Donnel, Mabel. New York: Harper & Row. Several difficulty levels. Twelve brief booklets with first-grade level "balloons" and more difficult signs.

*Button Family Adventures.* McCall, Edith. Chicago: Benefic Press. Preprimer through third-grade level. Twelve titles with stories of an "average" family. Interest through sixth grade.

*Core Vocabulary Readers.* Huber, Miriam B., et al. New York: Macmillan. Primer through third-grade levels. Outdoor interests; used with success for many years.

*Cowboy Sam Series.* Chandler, Edna Walker. Chicago: Benefic Press. Primer to third-grade difficulty. Eight books with simple but dramatic tales, mostly for boys. Interesting to eighth grade. Workbooks are available to accompany the readers; teacher's guide.

*Dan Frontier Series.* Hurley, William J. Chicago: Benefic Press. Preprimer level through third grade. Nine books. Interesting to eighth grade. Teacher's manual.

*Discovery Books.* Austin, Mary C. Champaign, Ill.: Garrard. About third-grade level. True biographies of American historical characters. Thirteen titles at this writing.

*Dolch Folklore of the World.* Dolch, E. W. Champaign, Ill.: Garrard. About third grade. Stories from Japan, Hawaii, Mexico, and several other countries available. Interest up to eighth grade.

*First Reading Books.* Dolch, E. W., and Dolch, M. P. Champaign, Ill.: Garrard. First grade. Stories of birds and animals, using easiest half of Basic Sight Vocabulary and Commonest Nouns.

*Frontiers of America Books.* McCall, Edith. Chicago: Children's Press. Third- to fourth-grade level. Stories of pioneers and explorers with interest to eighth grade. Mature format.

*Interesting Reading Series.* Botel, Morton. Chicago: Follett, 1960. Reading levels second through high third, but designed primarily for secondary school pupils. Nine titles and teacher's guide. A "Rapid Screening Test," presented in the front of each book, tests the pupil's ability to read.

*I Want to Be Series.* Greene, Carla. Chicago: Children's Press. Most at second- and third-grade difficulty. Career books for very slow readers, usable at least through eighth grade.

*Jerry Books.* Battle, Florence. Chicago: Benefic Press. Primer to third-grade level; interest to sixth grade.

*Jim Forest Series.* Rambeau, John, and Rambeau, Nancy. San Francisco: Harr-Wagner. Primer to third-grade level. Six books about a boy living with a forest ranger. Workbooks available with the first two in the series; teacher's manual.

*Junior Everyreader Series.* Kottmeyer, William. St. Louis: Webster. Third-grade difficulty. Simplified classics such as stories of Robin Hood and King Arthur.

*Little Owl, Wise Owl,* and *Young Owl Books.* Martin, Bill, Jr., ed. New York: Holt, Rinehart & Winston, 1964. Kindergarten through second-grade, second- through fourth-grade, and third-grade levels, respectively. Forty books in each set. Areas include social science, science, literature, and arithmetic.

*Morgan Bay Mysteries.* Rambeau, John, and Rambeau, Nancy. San Francisco: Harr-Wagner, 1961. Second- and third-grade difficulty. Four titles with interesting format and stories. Teacher's manual.

*Pleasure Reading Series.* Dolch, E. W., and Dolch, M. P. Champaign, Ill.: Garrard. Third-grade difficulty. Short stories based on classics, fairy tales, and folk tales. Interesting to sixth grade.

*Sailor Jack Series.* Wasserman, Selma, and Wasserman, Jack. Chicago: Benefic Press. Preprimer through third-grade level. Nine titles; most are very easy.

*Sport Readers.* Frissell, Bernice O., and Friebele, Mary L. New York: Macmillan. Second- and third-grade difficulty. Concerned with swimming, the playground, and the outdoors.

*True Books.* Chicago: Children's Press. Mostly third- and fourth-grade difficulty. Factual picture-stories by competent authors. Interesting through sixth grade.

*Wonder-Wonder Series.* Sharp, Adda Mai, and Young, Epsie. Austin, Tex.:

Steck. Preprimer through third-grade difficulty. Four books, close to primary in format and interest but with much fantasy.

### Difficulty Levels Fourth to Sixth Grade

*Allabout Books.* New York: Random House. Difficulty around fifth grade. About many things, mainly science or animal interests. Interest level through eighth grade.

*American Heritage Series.* Aladdin Books. New York: American Book Company. Fifth- and sixth-grade reading levels. American historical novels written in an easy style with many titles. Interesting to adults.

*Childhood of Famous Americans Series.* Indianapolis: Bobbs-Merrill. Fourth- to fifth-grade difficulty level. Over one hundred titles containing biographies of the childhood and youth of famous Americans. Interest at least through eighth grade.

*Everyreader Library.* Kottmeyer, William. St. Louis: Webster. Fourth- or low fifth-grade level. Simplified classics of interest to high-school level, especially *Cases of Sherlock Holmes* and *The Gold Bug.*

*First Book Series.* New York: Franklin Watts. Low third-grade level to sixth-grade level. Simple introductory books in the interest areas of science, animals, occupations. Factual and interesting even in high school.

*Junior Science Books.* Larrick, Nancy, ed. Champaign, Ill.: Garrard. Third- and fourth-grade difficulty. Well-illustrated.

*Landmark Books.* New York: Random House. Fourth- to eighth-grade levels. Over eighty titles; interesting through high school in the area of American history.

*Modern Adventure Stories.* Dressel, E. P., and Hirsch-Zeno, B. New York: Harper & Row. Paper covered. About fifth-grade difficulty. Mysterious with exciting plots; mature looking. Good through high-school level of interest.

*Reader's Digest Science Readers.* Pleasantville, N.Y.: Reader's Digest, Educational Division, 1961. Approximately fifth-grade level. Two books of interesting factual science articles and exploratory exercises; attractive format.

*Rivers of the World.* Larrick, Nancy, ed. Champaign, Ill.: Garrard, 1961–1962. Fifth-grade reading level. Five new books about the Amazon, Colorado, Mississippi, St. Lawrence, and Seine rivers. Interest up to the seventh grade.

*Simplified Classics.* Chicago: Scott, Foresman. Fourth- to fifth-grade difficulty. Differing and unusual formats. Interesting to high school.

*Stories for Teen-Agers.* Burton, Virginia, and Mersand, Joseph, eds. New York: Globe. Books 1 and 2. Fifth- and sixth-grade reading level. Short stories adapted from teen-age magazines.

*Teen-Age Tales.* Strang, Ruth. Boston: D. C. Heath. Books A, B, and 1 through 6. Fifth- and sixth-grade difficulty level. Short stories about things interesting to teen-agers with exercises and small teachers' guides. Interesting through high school.

*Terry and Bunky.* Fishel, Dick, et al. New York: G. P. Putnam's Sons. Third- to sixth-grade difficulty. Stories telling about the two boys learning a sport. Five titles with rules for the sport given in the appendix of each.

*Winston Adventure Series.* New York: Holt, Rinehart & Winston. Sixth- and seventh-grade levels. Fiction based on facts in American history, designed for junior high. Interesting through high school.

*Winston Science Fiction Novels.* New York: Holt, Rinehart & Winston. Sixth- and seventh-grade reading levels. Stories of science-fiction adventure, very interesting to present-day pupils.

*World Landmark Books.* New York: Random House. Fourth- through sixth-grade difficulty. Similar to *Landmark Books* but in European and Asian history.

*Young Readers Bookshelf.* New York: Lantern Press. Fifth- to seventh-grade reading levels. Collections of short stories in specific interest areas such as sports and mystery.

## Wide Spread of Difficulty Levels

*American Adventure Series.* Betts, Emmett. New York: Harper & Row. High second-grade through sixth-grade difficulty. Biographies of Indians, pioneers, trappers, pilots. Interesting through high school.

*The Deep Sea Adventure Series.* Berres, Frances, et al. San Francisco: Harr-Wagner. Difficulty levels from low second to about fifth grade. Exciting content, appropriate slate-blue illustrations. Mature appearance. Very interesting even to high school.

*Ginn Enrichment Readers.* Boston: Ginn, 1962. Level shown following the title: *Come With Me* (primer); *Under the Apple Tree* (1); *Open the Gate* (2); *Ranches and Rainbows* (3); *Fun and Fancy* (4); *Down Story Roads* (5); *Along Story Trails* (6); *On Story Wings* (7). Each with carefully controlled vocabulary.

*Reader's Digest Reading Skill Builders.* Thomas, Lydia, et al. Pleasantville, N.Y.: Reader's Digest Educational Division. Three sets available for grades two through six; two sets for grades seven and eight. Adapted from the adult *Reader's Digest,* so interest is very high. Carefully developed exercises for most stories.

*Reading Essentials Series.* Leavell, Ullin, et al. Austin, Tex.: Steck. Level shown following title: *Come and Play* (1); *Fun Time* (2); *Play Time* (3); *New Goals in Reading* (Remedial 3–6); *New Avenues in Reading*

(4) ; *New Journeys in Reading* (5) ; *New Adventures in Reading* (6) ; *Progress in Reading* (7) ; *Mastery in Reading* (8). Workbook-practice materials, some in color. Vocabulary control, some quite easy. Many exercises in phonetic and structural analysis. Teaching aids and games also available.

*SRA Whitman Classroom Bookshelf.* Chicago: Science Research Associates, 1962. Fourth- to ninth-grade level: Science (Learn About Science), grades four to seven; social studies (Badger), grades four to seven; classics (Whitman Classics Series), grades four to nine. Set of forty-four volumes; attractive and reasonably priced.

*Woodland Frolics Series.* Sharp, Adda Mai, and Young, Epsie. Austin, Tex.: Steck. From preprimer through sixth-grade difficulty. About animals and their various adventures, beautifully illustrated in vivid color.

Many other books are available. In addition to consulting the latest lists, teachers should write to the publishers (on school stationery) asking for information on their latest publications of this type. Many titles are available in paperback, or are found in special collections designed to motivate and attract the reader.

For information on periodicals for boys and girls, see:

Dallmann, Martha, et al. *The Teaching of Reading.* 4th ed. New York: Holt, Rinehart & Winston, 1974, pp. 572–76.

# 9 SELECTING TEXTBOOKS

## THE PROBLEM

A major problem facing every administrator and teacher is that of book selection. The enormous range of reading ability and interest found in a regular classroom has already been discussed. But even though the reading level of the students is known and there is sufficient curricular flexibility to allow choices in materials, teachers sometimes still have difficulty determining the approximate readability of books. This is especially true of teachers at higher grade levels and in the secondary schools where texts are used more and where the teacher is largely concerned with a subject area. This section, therefore, is primarily addressed to the content-area teacher.

Commonly used content textbooks are quite often written at a higher level of readability than the grade level in which they are employed. Much depends upon the background of the reader in the field being taught.

For an eye-opening example, select three textbooks from the shelves of your school in three fields unrelated to your own specialization, and read a page in the center of each book. (English teachers should try advanced algebra or physics; physical science teachers might attempt texts in poetry or grammar.) Read them one after another as students might in studying their homework for one evening. If you, as a reader, have at least a partial background in any of the areas of study, the reading level of the material should be relatively simple. If you do not, you may be in much the same difficulty as many conscientious students. The vocabulary problems are considerable, the sentence structure seems unnecessarily complex, and the ideas do not seem to be clearly presented. And if this is true for a good reader, think of the problems the below-average reader has!

You may find, in your samples, that one or more of the authors define words in context, use relatively simple sentences, and tend to use nontechnical words wherever possible to describe a new technical process or concept. If so, the readability level of that material will be lower than those that use complex sentence structure and technical vocabulary that is either undefined except in a glossary or defined in an involved textbook way. This may happen with books in English grammar, in biological or physical science, in mathematics, or even in industrial arts or physical education. Authors who are not conscious of readability may be found in any field—the important thing is the teacher's consciousness of the problem.

In your own field, you are likely to be less conscious of the difficulty. Since you know all the words well and have dealt with the concepts previously, it will seem simple to you. When you move to unfamiliar territory, however, you approximate the feelings of a pupil meeting this field for the first time.

Because determining difficulty level of materials to be used is a continuing problem and because selection of materials is often controlled by content teachers, this section will discuss briefly how to determine the approximate reading level of printed materials.

## A DEFINITION OF READABILITY

Readability is the relation of the level of the printed material to the reading ability of the students. Readable books are those with qualities that fit the ability of the students for whom they are intended. Readability depends on such factors as legibility, interest, and ease of understanding.

### Legibility

Legibility is affected by size of type, length of line, spacing between lines, color and kind of paper, color of ink, width of margins, and style of typeface. Many studies of these factors have been completed.

In general, teachers who are choosing books should be conscious of the following major factors:

1.   A double-column page seems to be more legible and to afford greater ease of eye movement than a page with a single column extending across the full width.

2.   Typeface must be ten or twelve points in size to be read easily by most students. (This book is set in ten-point type.)

3.   Black printing on white *dull-finish* paper provides optimum legibility.

4.   Considerable spacing between lines of print and full margins are advantageous.

For complete information, see:

Tinker, Miles A. *Legibility of Print.* Ames, Iowa: Iowa State University Press, 1963.

### Interest and Ease of Understanding

A previous chapter has already noted how interest and ease of reading rise and decline together. In general, reading ability can be expected to rise by as much as two full grades if the reader's interest is high.

The factors contributing to the difficulty or ease of written material have been subjected to a great deal of research during the last thirty years. Formulas for the estimation of reading difficulty usually include the following factors:

Number of different words in a sample

Number of prepositions in the sample

Number of words in the sample that do not appear in Thorndike's list of 10,000 words (or Dale's list of 769 words or of 3000 words, or some other list of commonly used words)

Number of simple sentences

Percentage of difficult words in relation to a given list or as gauged by the number of syllables in the words

Sentence length

Number of abstract words

Number of prefixes and suffixes

## FORMULAS TO ESTIMATE READABILITY

As more research has been accomplished, comparable results have been achieved by using formulas that are simpler in application. Most teachers are not concerned with absolute readability levels, but want a quick approximation that is readily usable.

For teachers wishing to estimate readability of primary-level materials, the *Spache formula* is suggested.[1] The *Lorge formula* is useful for difficulty ranges from fourth to eighth grade, but is difficult and time consuming to use.[2] The *Dale-Chall formula*, which is probably the one most widely used by publishers but which takes some time to apply, is applicable from about fifth-grade to college level.[3] Perhaps an easier formula to apply above sixth-grade difficulty is the *Flesch formula*.[4] (Flesch's earlier works on the formula are most useful for those considering writing for publication or rewriting for classroom use; his last work deals directly with readability, both in terms of difficulty and interest.)

For purposes of demonstrating how formulas work to estimate read-

[1] George D. Spache, *Good Reading for Poor Readers* (Champaign, Ill.: Garrard, 1972).

[2] Irving Lorge, "Predicting Reader Difficulty of Selections for Children," *Elementary English Review* 16 (October 1939), 229–33; and "Predicting Readability," *Teachers College Board* 40 (March 1944), 404–19.

[3] Dale, Edgar, and Chall, Jeanne, "A Formula for Predicting Readability," *Educational Research Bulletin* 27 (January 21 and February 17, 1948), 11–20, 37–54. Also available in pamphlet form.

[4] Rudolph Flesch, *The Art of Plain Talk* (New York: Harper & Row, 1946); *The Art of Readable Writing* (New York: Harper & Row, 1949); and *How to Test Readability* (New York: Harper & Row, 1951).

ability, a very simple one, the *Fry formula*, has been chosen.[5] The directions for applying the Fry formula are:

1. Select three 100-word passages from near the beginning, middle, and end of the book. Ignore all proper nouns.

2. Count the total number of sentences in each passage, estimating to the nearest tenth of a sentence. Average the three numbers from the three passages.

3. Count the total number of syllables in each 100-word sample. (There is a syllable for each vowel sound.) Or, for convenience, count every syllable over one in each word and add 100. Average these three numbers.

4. Locate on the graph shown the average number of sentences per 100 words and the average number of syllables per 100 words. Most plot points will be near the heavy curved line. The approximate grade levels are marked off by the lines intersecting the heavy curved line.

5. If great variability in the three samples is observed, choose a greater number of samples.

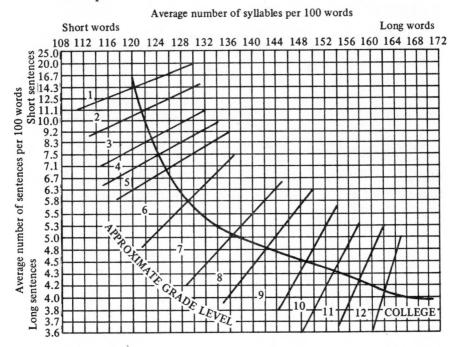

To avoid even this simple arithmetic, there is a device on the market called the Reading Ease Calculator. It is a pocket-sized plastic device developed by the Employee Research Section of General Motors Corporation and obtainable through Science Research Associates to measure the difficulty of

[5] Edward Fry, "A Readability Formula That Saves Time," *Journal of Reading* 11 (April 1968), 513–16, 575–78.

printed material. The calculator uses word length and sentence structure as basic elements for gauging readability. As these elements are manipulated in accord with directions provided in the accompanying manual, readability ranges are indicated by a revolving color wheel. Use of this calculator gives what is probably the fastest method of obtaining an estimate of readability, and the results are presented in general ranges rather than grades and tenths of grades (which sometimes give a false sense of accuracy to the results). On the other hand, results are likely to be even less accurate than those achieved by some of the formulas mentioned above because the estimate is more general and not so closely tied to common words now in use.

For more on measuring readability, see:

Gunning, Robert. *The Technique of Clear Writing*. Rev. ed. New York: McGraw-Hill, 1968.

## AN INFORMAL APPROACH TO ESTIMATING READABILITY

Even without using a readability formula, a teacher can make some rough estimates of reading difficulty and eliminate some problem books immediately. If the sentences are long, the syntax involved, the words unusual or highly technical without explanation in context, or if the book appears "packed" either in typography or in format, it should probably not be considered. A book intended to present something new to a student should attract, not repel or discourage.

It is often helpful to "try on books for size" with a few typical students to see what difficulties are common and which books are preferred by them. After all, it is better for the book to suit those trying to learn from it, rather than the person who already knows the subject—the teacher. Too often teachers take the opposite approach.

# $10$ TESTING IN READING

Much of the curricular choice of teachers must be based on a knowledge of the reading levels of individuals and groups in the classroom. Classes vary from period to period in a departmentalized situation, and even in a self-contained classroom, teaching is impossible unless there is understanding of the range and type of reading skill present. Could a group be formed within the classroom where all are operating on the same level or need the same kind of help? Which of the available textbooks is the most likely to be the "right" one for this class? What are the specific problems—vocabulary, comprehension, word attack, speed? In short, unless the teaching situation is known, the selection is more likely to produce problems than genuine learning.

Information as to the reading skills of individuals and groups may be obtained quickly through informal and formal testing. This chapter begins with the more informal approaches and moves to a listing and explanation of standardized group tests. Later test selection, testing policies, and test interpretation in regard to standardized instruments are discussed.

Formal individual testing of reading is not covered here because time is required away from the classroom by both teacher and student in order to do the testing and most content-area teachers do not attempt it. However, the informal methods do provide a partial substitute that can be used, and references shown will give information on individual testing of reading for those who desire such information.

## INFORMAL TESTING OF READING LEVEL

One procedure that can be used for groups or individuals in informal classroom testing operates as follows:

1. Obtain copies of available books that deal with the subject matter of the course. (A single copy of the different books is sufficient for individ-

ual testing with the teacher looking on; if the book is to be passed around the class, the teacher should probably have his or her own copy.) Arrange the books from "easy" to "difficult."

2.    Starting with the easiest book, have each pupil read a paragraph (or at least five lines) orally.

3.    If a pupil encounters an unknown word, allow about three seconds and supply the word. When he or she reads a word incorrectly, correct the mistake if it is one of mispronunciation or if it affects meaning. (Mistakes on some small words, such as *a* and *the*, do not affect meaning to any degree.)

4.    Keep a tally of these problems for each pupil; note the number and, if possible, the kinds of errors he or she makes.

5.    Determine which of the following three levels the student is operating on for each book:

   a.    *Independent level.* The pupil finds not more than one unknown word in each one hundred consecutive words (errors less than 1 percent). Oral reading is natural, somewhat rhythmical, and well phrased. Expression shows understanding of the concepts.

   b.    *Instructional level.* The pupil finds two to four unknown words in each one hundred consecutive words (errors 2 to 4 percent). Oral reading is still well phrased and natural and few tensions are evident. There are occasional problems with expression because the pupil experiences some slight difficulty in understanding and fluency.

   c.    *Frustration level.* The pupil misses five or more words per one hundred consecutive words (errors 5 percent or more). Oral reading becomes jerky, repetitive, and word-by-word. Tensions show in wriggling, frowning, faulty breath control, or high tone of voice.

6.    To add comprehension testing to the task, prepare four varied comprehension questions for each selection and ask these after the oral reading is completed by each pupil. Questions should test direct recall of facts as well as inference and organization. Comprehension at independent level should be almost perfect (90 percent or better), at instructional level about 75 percent, and at the frustration level less than 75 percent.

7.    Proceed upward through the books, excusing pupils from reading the more difficult books when it becomes apparent that they have reached the frustration level.

This procedure may be used with readers as well as with content books. When applied to readers that are graded, each student's reading capacity can be assigned a "grade-level equivalent" from one through eight for each of the three levels.

This informal determination provides an analysis of both the general class level and particular problems present. It can be the basis for grouping. It certainly gives a usable estimate of the probable curricular content and difficulty as well as the suitability of several books in the content area.

Teaching should not be attempted at the frustration level, at least if books are the principal teaching medium. Pupils cannot be taught to read better using frustration-level books, and they also will have difficulty learning content presented at this level. No one can learn if the load is too great. On the other hand, pupils can learn very little if they read continually at the independent level. In reading classes, the book at the instructional level is the only one that provides the requisites for real learning.

For more information on informal procedures, see:

Austin, Mary C., Bush, Clifford L., and Huebner, Mildred H. *Reading Evaluation.* New York: The Ronald Press, 1961, pp. 12–16, 235–46.

Bond, Guy L., and Tinker, Miles A. *Reading Difficulties: Their Diagnosis and Correction.* 3rd ed. New York: Appleton-Century-Crofts, 1973, pp. 220–26.

LaPray, Margaret. *Teaching Children to Become Independent Readers.* New York: The Center for Applied Research in Education, 1972, pp. 62–72.

Smith, Nila B. *Graded Selections for Informal Reading Diagnosis: Grades One Through Three.* New York: University Press, 1959.

————. *Graded Selections for Informal Reading Diagnosis: Grades Four through Six.* New York: University Press, 1963.

## STANDARDIZED GROUP TESTS OF READING

Table 10.1 that follows shows the most commonly used group tests of reading skills and abilities and Table 10.2 following that lists common individual tests. For more information on any of these tests, write the publishers indicated in the tables and listed on page 121, or consult the *Mental Measurements Yearbook.*[1]

Many of the tests yield scores for subtests not specifically mentioned below due to space limitations. The general categories tested are shown with grade levels for which the tests are intended. Many of these tests have been revised (some several times) since the original year of publication listed.

[1] Oscar K. Buros, ed., *Mental Measurements Yearbook* (Highland Park, N.J.: Gryphon ress, revised every few years).

**TABLE 10.1**
**GROUP READING TESTS AND READING-RELATED TESTS***

| Name of Test | General Abilities Measured | For Grades | Approx. Time (min.) | Number of Forms | Publisher and Year (see address list) |
|---|---|---|---|---|---|
| American School Achievement Tests: Reading | Vocabulary, comprehension | 1, 2–3, 4–6, 7–9, 10–13 | 25 | 3 or 4 | BM 1955 |
| Brown-Carlsen Listening Comprehension Test | Recall, following directions, transitions, vocabulary, lecture comprehension | 9–13 | 50 | 2 | HBJ |
| Buffalo Reading Test for Speed and Comprehension | Rate, comprehension | 7–16 | | 2 | FS 1941 |
| California Phonics Survey | Phonics (8 scores) | 1, 2, 3, 4, 4–6, 7–9, 9–14 | 50 | 2 | CTB 1963 |
| California Reading Test | Vocabulary, comprehension | 1–3, 4–6, 7–9, 9–14 | 20–50 | 4 | CTB 1957 |
| Chicago Reading Tests | Comprehension rate (all except 1–2), reading maps and graphs (4–6, 6–8) | 1–2, 2–4, 4–6, 6–8 | 45 | 3 | EMH 1940 |
| Comprehensive Tests of Basic Skills: Reading and Study Skills | Vocabulary, comprehension; study: references and graphs | 2.5–4 4–6, 6–8, 8–12 | 11, 30, 10, 19 | 2 | CTB 1968 |
| Cooperative Dictionary Test | Alphabetizing, spelling, pronunciation, meaning | 7–12 | 30 | 1 | ETS |
| Cooperative Reading Comprehension | Vocabulary, speed of comprehension, level of comprehension | 7–10 10–14 | 40 | 4 | ETS 1952 |
| Detroit Reading Tests | Rate, comprehension | 2–3, 4–6, 7–9 | 8 | 4 | HBJ 1927 |

| Name of Test | General Abilities Measured | For Grades | Approx. Time (min.) | Number of Forms | Publisher and Year (see address list) |
|---|---|---|---|---|---|
| Developmental Reading Tests: Primary and Intermediate | Vocabulary, comprehension (several types) Appreciation | Primer, L. Primary, U. Primary, 4–6 | 45<br><br><br>32 | 1 | L&C |
| Diagnostic Reading Tests | Survey: rate, vocabulary, comprehension Diagnostic: vocabulary, comprehension, rate, word attack | K–4, 4–8, 7–13 | 40<br><br><br>15–60 | 2<br><br><br>8 | SRA 1952 |
| Doren Diagnostic Reading Test | Word recognition | 1–12 | 180 | 1 | ETS |
| Durost-Center Word Mastery Test | Word meanings: isolated and in context | 9–13 | 100 | 2 | HBJ |
| Dvorak-Van Wagenen Diagnostic Examination of Silent Reading Abilities | Rate of comprehension, vocabulary, range of information, comprehension | 4–6, 7–9, 10–12 | Untimed | 1 | VW |
| Gates Basic Reading Test | Vocabulary, comprehension (several types) | 3.5–8 | 70 | 4 | TCP |
| Gates Reading Survey | Speed and accuracy, vocabulary, comprehension | 3–10 | 60–90 | 3 | TCP 1958 |
| Haggerty Reading Examination | Vocabulary, comprehension | 1–3, 6–12 | 20–28 | 1 | HBJ |
| Iowa Every-Pupil Test of Basic Skills | Vocabulary, comprehension, study skills (several types) | 3–5, 5–9 | 46, 85 | 4 | HM 1940–47 |
| Iowa Silent Reading Test | Comprehension rate, vocabulary, locational skills | 4–8, 9–13 | 45–60 | 4 | HBJ 1956 |

| Name of Test | General Abilities Measured | For Grades | Approx. Time (min.) | Number of Forms | Publisher and Year (see address list) |
|---|---|---|---|---|---|
| Iowa Tests of Educational Development | Comprehension in social studies, natural sciences | 9–13 | 60 | 2 | SRA 1958 |
| Kelley-Greene Reading Comprehension Test | Comprehension rate, directed reading | 9–12 | 63 | 3 | HBJ 1955 |
| Los Angeles Primary or Elementary Reading Tests | Comprehension | 1–3, 3–9 | 10, 30 | 4 | CTB |
| McCullough Word Analysis Tests | Phonetic analysis, structural analysis (7 tests) | 4–13 | Untimed | 1 | PP 1962 |
| Metropolitan Achievement Tests: Reading | Vocabulary, comprehension | 1–2, 3–4, 5–7.5, 7–9.5 | 35–60 | 3 | HBJ |
| Michigan Speed of Reading Test | Rate | 6–16 | 7 | 2 | PC |
| Monroe Revised Silent Reading Tests | Rate, comprehension | 3–5, 6–8, 9–12 | 5 | 3 | PSP |
| National Achievement Test: Reading | Directions, comprehension, rate | 3–6, 6–8 | 33 | 2 | APC |
| Nelson-Denny Reading Test | Vocabulary, paragraph reading | 10–14 | 30 | 2 | HM 1929 |
| Nelson Silent Reading Test | Vocabulary, comprehension | 3–9 | 30 | 2 | HM |
| Prescriptive Reading Inventory | Phonic and structural analysis, vocabulary, comprehension (90 objectives) | 1.5–2.5, 2.0–3.5, 3.0–4.5, 4.0–6.5 | 150 | 1 | CTB 1972 |
| Sangren-Woody Reading Test | Rate, comprehension (several types), Directions, Organization | 4–8 | 27 | 2 | HBJ |

| Name of Test | General Abilities Measured | For Grades | Approx. Time (min.) | Number of Forms | Publisher and Year (see address list) |
|---|---|---|---|---|---|
| Scholastic Diagnostic Reading Test | Vocabulary, comprehension, study skills, word recognition | 1–3, 4–6, 7–9 | 60 | 2 | STS 1955 |
| Schrammel-Gray High School and College Reading Test | Comprehension rate | 7–13 | 25 | 2 | PSP 1940 |
| Sequential tests of Educational Progress: Reading | Comprehension | 4–6, 7–9, 10–12, 13–14 | 70 | 2 | ETS 1957 |
| Silent Reading Diagnostic Test | Word recognition, analysis, synthesis, and word parts | 2.5–6 | 90 | 1 | L&C |
| SRA Achievement Tests: Reading | Verbal-pictorial association, language perception, comprehension, vocabulary | 1–2, 2–4, 4–6, 6–9 | 45–60 | 2 | SRA 1955 |
| SRA Reading Record | Comprehension, vocabulary, basic skills, rate | 7–12 | 40 | 1 | SRA 1947 |
| Stanford Diagnostic Reading Test | Comprehension, vocabulary, auditory discrimination, phonics, syllabication, rate | 2–4, 5–8 | Untimed | 2 | HBJ |
| Stanford Reading Tests | Comprehension, vocabulary | 1, 2–3, 4–6, 7–9 | 30–40 | 3–5 | HBJ |
| Test on the Use of Books and Libraries | Use of library and reference sources | 7–12 | 50 | 2 | ETS |
| Tests of Natural Sciences: Vocabulary and Interpretation of Reading Materials | Vocabulary, interpretation | 8–13 | 35 | 2 | ETS |

| Name of Test | General Abilities Measured | For Grades | Approx. Time (min.) | Number of Forms | Publisher and Year (see address list) |
|---|---|---|---|---|---|
| Tests of Social Studies: Vocabulary and Interpretation of Reading Materials | Vocabulary, interpretation | 8–13 | 35 | 2 | ETS |
| Traxler Silent Reading Test | Word meaning, comprehension, rate | 7–10 | 46 | 4 | BM 1942 |
| Van Wagenen Analytical Reading Scales | Comprehension | 4–6, 7–9, 10–12 | Untimed | 1 | VW |
| Van Wagenen Comprehensive Reading Scales | Comprehension | 4–12 | Untimed | 1 | VW |
| Van Wagenen Listening Vocabulary Scale | Listening vocabulary | 2–6 | Untimed | 1 | VW |

* For more complete listings of reading tests, see Roger Farr, *Reading: What Can Be Measured?* (Newark, Del.: International Reading Association, 1969), pp. 228–65.

**TABLE 10.2**

**INDIVIDUAL READING AND READING-RELATED TESTS***

| Name of Test | General Abilities Measured | For Grades | Number of Forms | Publisher and Year (see address list) |
|---|---|---|---|---|
| Auditory Discrimination Test | Auditory discrimination | all | 2 | LRA 1958 |
| Botel Reading Inventory | Phonics, word recognition, word opposites | 1–12 | 2 | F 1966 |
| Diagnostic Reading Scales | Word recognition, oral and silent reading, auditory comprehension | 1–8 | 1 | CTB 1963 |
| Durrell Analysis of Reading Difficulty | Oral and silent reading, listening comprehension, word recognition and analysis, naming, identifying and matching letters, visual memory and hearing sounds in words, sounds of letters, learning rate, phonic spelling, spelling test, handwriting | 1–6 | 1 | HBJ 1955 |
| Frostig Developmental Test of Visual Perception | Eye-motor coordination, figure-ground, constancy of shape, position in space, spatial relationships | Ages 4–8 | 1 | F |
| Gates-McKillop Reading Diagnostic Tests | Mispronunciation, omissions, additions, repetitions, words and phrases, word parts, names of sounds and letters, blending, spelling, oral vocabulary, syllabication, auditory discrimination | 2–6 | 2 | TCP 1962 |
| Gilmore Oral Reading Test | Accuracy, rate, comprehension | 1–8 | 2 | HBJ 1968 |
| Gray Oral Reading Test | Oral reading, comprehension | 1–16+ | 4 | BM 1967 |
| Harris Tests of Lateral Dominance | Eye, hand, and foot dominance | 1–adult | 1 | PC |

| Name of Test | General Abilities Measured | For Grades | Number of Forms | Publisher and Year (see address list) |
|---|---|---|---|---|
| Keystone Visual Survey Tests | Visual functioning | 1–adult | 1 | KEY |
| Oral Reading Criterion Test | Oral reading | 1–7 | 1 | D |
| Phonics Knowledge Criterion Test | Phonics, (phoneme-grapheme correspondence) | 1–6 | 1 | D |
| Phonics Knowledge Survey | Phonics | 1–8 | 1 | TCP |
| Roswell-Chall Diagnostic Reading Test of Word Analysis Skills | Phonics, syllabication | 2–6 | 2 | E |
| Standard Reading Inventory | Vocabulary, oral and silent reading, comprehension, rate | 1–8 | 2 | K |

* For more complete listings of reading tests, see Roger Farr, *Reading: What Can Be Measured?* (Newark, Del.: International Reading Association, 1969), pp. 228–65.

## ADDRESSES OF PUBLISHERS

NOTE: Letters given before certain publishers in this list refer to the abbreviations used in Tables 10.1 and 10.2.

APC  Acorn Publishing Company
Rockville Centre, N.Y. 11570

BM  Bobbs-Merrill Co., Test
Division
4300 West 62nd Street
Indianapolis, Ind. 46206

CTB  California Test Bureau
Del Monte Research Park
Monterey, Calif. 93940

D  Drier Educational Systems
320 Raritan Avenue
Highland Park, N.J. 08904

ETS  Educational Testing Service
Cooperative Test Division
Princeton, N.J. 08540

EMH  E. M. Hale and Company
1201 South Hastings Way
Eau Claire, Wis. 54701

E  Essay Press
P.O. Box 5, Planetarium
Station
New York, N.Y. 10024

F  Follett Publishing Company
1010 West Washington
Boulevard
Chicago, Ill. 60607

FS  Foster and Stewart
Publishing Company
Buffalo, N.Y.

HBJ  Harcourt Brace Jovanovich
757 Third Avenue
New York, N.Y. 10017

HM  Houghton Mifflin Company
2 Park Street
Boston, Mass. 02107

KEY  Keystone View Company
Meadville, Pa. 16335

K  Klamath Printing Company
320 Lowell
Klamath Falls, Ore. 97601

LRA  Language Research Associates
300 North State Street
Chicago, Ill. 60610

L&C  Lyons and Carnahan
407 East 25th Street
Chicago, Ill. 60616

PP  Personnel Press
180 Nassau Street
Princeton, N.J. 08540

PC  The Psychological Corporation
304 East 45th Street
New York, N.Y. 10017

PSP  Public School Publishing
Company
204 West Mulberry Street
Bloomington, Ill. 61701

STS  Scholastic Testing Service
480 Meyer Road
Bensenville, Ill. 60166

SRA  Science Research Associates
259 East Erie Street
Chicago, Ill. 60611

TCP  Teachers College Press
Columbia University
525 West 120th Street
New York, N.Y. 10027

VW  Van Wagenen Psyco-
Educational Research
Laboratories
1729 Irving Avenue, South
Minneapolis, Minn. 55405

## SELECTION OF TESTS

In choosing tests for use in evaluating reading performance, there are a number of considerations. No test can fulfill all expectations, but time should be spent in choosing the test that fits a particular district's needs best. Test publishing companies sell specimen sets at cost for perusal. Even after careful examination, usage may reveal that the test does not come up to expectations.

When choosing a test the following questions should be asked:

1.   Is the test valid, that is, does it measure what it purports to measure? Does it sample widely or concentrate on only a few skills? Do the scores show how individuals and groups are reading?

2.   Can the test be administered and scored easily? (The amount of testing time should be the last consideration since whether it can be given in one period is not nearly as important as other aspects.) Are the directions clear to pupils, and the scoring directions clear to teachers?

3.   Do the scores indicate strengths and weaknesses clearly? Could the results be understood and interpreted by the pupils? Are the parts specific enough that the teacher would know what to teach in view of the weaknesses noted?

4.   Is the test reliable? (If not, then using this particular instrument as a pre- and posttest is out of the question.)

5.   Are the kinds of items familiar to the children being tested, or are they phrased in strange ways, concerned with obscure things, or otherwise not clear?

Many reading tests do not show progress in the specific materials that have been studied, simply because the test itself does not attempt to cover these materials. Tests are very short samples of behavior, and in order to achieve a short sample, many possible types of exercises or questions must be left out. This, of course, is why test results are not enough in evaluating students. Standardized tests do not measure motivation, interest in reading, attitude toward reading, appreciation, or creative and critical reading. All these factors may have a great deal to do with level of achievement. Even more specific knowledge may not be tested in a particular test. In choosing tests, teachers should be certain that the test fits the curriculum and they should avoid assuming that the test score adequately measures the entire reading program.

Tests must be carefully administered; results must be interpreted with care; clearly defined policies of reporting the results are needed. The aim of testing is to improve instruction, and this aim should not be obscured by the reporting of test results. Giving the test, scoring the test, and tabulating the results are only preliminary steps. The last steps—evaluating the results and then attacking the problems—are the only things that make the first three steps worthwhile.

But the first steps are important. On the basis of the questions posed above, the following evaluative procedures for test selection are recommended:

1.   Determine ahead of time the educational objectives for which you wish to test. Check the test item by item to see whether all items are consistent with your objectives and appropriate to your pupils.

2.   Check the reliability given for the test. In most cases reliabilities of .85 and above are adequate, but the higher the better.

3.   Read the directions for administering the test and the directions for scoring, if this is to be done by teachers. Determine whether these directions are clear enough for all concerned.

4.   Examine the format of the test. It should be attractive, easy to see, and up to date. If there are pictures, they should be clear.

5.   Investigate the publisher. The company should be able to render assistance in person or by mail if problems occur. Check to see if supplementary materials published with help in interpretation or use of the results are available.

6.   Determine whether or not this is one of a series of tests, or a "loner." In achievement testing, particularly, it is important to have a longitudinal series so that comparable measurements may be made at succeeding grade levels.

7.   Look at the norms. They should be established on a large, representative population and the characteristics of that group with whom your pupils will be compared should be known.

8.   Consider the record forms, the manual, and any other services available. The forms should reveal the type of comparisons easily made and whether individual problems can be located rapidly. If scoring services are provided, the forms should lend themselves to easy reading. An accompanying manual that gives specific suggestions is usually very helpful. Machine checking, recording, and profiling are usually a plus factor.

9.   See what happens to the test scores. Students should be able to get a profile of their strengths and weaknesses and class summaries should be available for the teacher. The most useful tests reveal specific difficulties so that something may be done about them.

## POLICIES BEFORE AND DURING TESTING

The results of any test are always subject to question, since any emotional, physical, or environmental circumstance can affect the performance of individuals to a considerable degree. If test results are to be most useful, the testing situation must be optimum. A few cautions seem in order.

First, it is probably best for a school district to use the same testing instrument for several years so that interpretation of the results can be more accurate. All tests have their pecularities. After one or two years of use a test is always better understood, more accurately interpreted by all concerned, and the results put to better use. The newest test is not always the best test, and if a child's cumulative record shows many changes from one test to another in the same area (as in reading), the progress of the individual may be almost impossible to determine. On the other hand, it is foolish to continue using a test simply because it has been used before, without careful analysis of what this test has accomplished and how other instruments might be more applicable. In general, then, a particular test should be used over a span of several years before replacement by another that appears to be better.

Second, a qualitative analysis, if possible, is usually more helpful to teachers than a quantitative analysis. It is important to know that Joseph is reading at 3.2 level, certainly, but the more important question is: "What are the factors that are causing him to read at 3.2 grade level?" An analysis of relative strengths and weaknesses will better show how to help him improve.

Third, even though some of the statements in the manual of a standardized test may appear ridiculous, they must be followed *to the letter*. The procedure in giving a standardized test is part of the standardization of that test—any deviation from this procedure will invalidate the scores. This is especially difficult for some teachers to do since testing is so different from teaching. Repeating the directions, allowing extra time for a slow child, giving a hint to the child who almost has the answer, introducing extra examples before the test, or any special procedure for the group or for individuals removes the basis for comparison. And a broader basis for comparison is the major advantage offered by the national norms of a standardized test. The teacher or administrator, through a standardized test, can compare his or her classroom or school with a nationwide sample. But unless the test is administered as the manual states, one of the standards is removed, and the scores become less meaningful.

Besides following these general pretest policies, there are some practical matters to be considered. For instance, it is not ordinarily a good policy to administer tests just before or just after a vacation. Children, at these times, will not perform as adequately as they can under ordinary circumstances. Just prior to a vacation they are anxious to finish up and be on their way. This means they are not likely to do as thorough a job as they ordinarily would. Testing immediately following a vacation will also tend to produce lowered scores since pupils are simply not "with it" yet. The same problem applies for a somewhat different reason when administering tests immediately following a period of physical education or other strenuous activity.

Some thought should also be given to preparing for the test. The test manual should always be studied carefully before a test is attempted and *not* during the time it is being administered. Gross errors sometimes occur this way. It is a good policy to rehearse oral directions *aloud*, and note the time that they take when given in this fashion. Teachers often fail to allow enough time simply because they have rehearsed the procedure utilizing silent reading instead of oral reading. It is even sensible for the teacher to take the test prior to the group administration since this may show the problems that pupils are likely to have.

Preparing students for the test is equally important. Tests should not be made too *special*. If they are made to seem too important, students may develop tensions that will prevent their doing well. Treating tests matter-of-factly, as if they were daily lessons, is a good rule since one is really no more important than the other. For any test, however, plenty of pencils, erasers, scratch paper, or whatever is necessary should be immediately available. This becomes quite important if the test has short time limits, but it can even be a distraction on an untimed test.

One of the greatest distractions that can occur during the administration of a test is that of adult voices. Since pupils are attuned to adult voices for their teaching, they will tend to pay attention to the voices rather than the test, and the test results will suffer. If it becomes necessary for the teacher to speak to the principal, for example, during the administration of a test, this should be done quietly out in the hall rather than within the testing room. Most psychometrists will put a sign on the door stating "Testing—Do Not Disturb" to avoid distractions.

The physical aspects of the room must be checked to see that such factors as light and heat are normal. Especially with younger children, teachers must make certain that physical needs are taken care of first. In addition, provisions may need to be made for special cases such as left-handed children. The test materials should be handled as easily by a left-handed pupil as by a right-handed pupil.

After completion of the testing, papers should always be checked for the correctness of information required (birth date, age, name). An intelligence test score, for example, may be completely invalidated by an incorrect birth date.

Some of these precautions may seem relatively minor but each is sufficiently vital so that a breach may seriously undermine the effectiveness of a test.

## CRITERION-REFERENCED TESTS

The newest form of test is the criterion-referenced test. It is an inventory (a thorough measurement of a limited skill area) which samples desired student behaviors in a particular area of study. Students are compared in their responses to expected behavior. That is, their mastery (or lack of mastery) of particular behaviors specified by an objective is measured. The scores indicate how much they know in terms of a specific behavioral objective.

Though sometimes contrasted with standardized norm-referenced tests, there are many areas of overlap between the two. A norm-referenced test also samples behavior in an area of study. One difference is that the sampling in norm-referenced tests will ordinarily be broader, and mastery is not expected. (As a matter of fact, unless there are some questions which cannot be answered by the student, the student's ability probably has not been completely tested.) Another difference is that norm-referencing compares students to others like them in age and grade, not to a preordained objective to be attained.

But both types of test do begin with objectives, and both make a comparison. Objectives may be behaviorally stated in both, though they tend to be less specific in norm-referenced tests. Criterion-referenced tests tend to have a greater number of items to cover an area of knowledge and to be administered in smaller portions of that area of knowledge than do normed tests. Items in criterion-referenced tests are also likely to be less discriminating per item, but ordinarily expect a certain level of performance (90 percent or some other standard) before "mastery" of the objective is assumed.

Basically, criterion-referenced testing (called by other names) has been employed by teachers in teacher-made tests as long as there have been classrooms. Oral reading tests are essentially criterion-referenced; so are informal reading inventories. Choice of a criterion-referenced over a norm-referenced test is, therefore, a question of purpose, and both are needed in many cases. Criterion-referenced tests are usually best in adjusting day-to-day instruction to particular learning needs of individual children.

The following questions may give some direction to choices:

1.  Does the test have several forms so the children can be checked on *new* questions concerned with the same specific skill, rather than achieving the correct answers through familiarity?

2.  Is there provision for later assessment after forgetting occurs? (Forgetting is universal; review is very important.)

3.  Is "mastery" defined sensibly? (Perfection is a large order!)

4.  Are the objectives so specific that transfer fails to occur? Or is reading treated as a more unitary skill?

5.  Is too much time spent in testing rather than teaching? Or, on the other hand, is one of the major objectives to produce confidence in test-taking, so performance is higher during a testing situation?

For more information on this type of testing, see:

Blanton, William E., et al., eds. *Measuring Reading Performance.* Newark, Del.: International Reading Association, 1974.

*Interpretive Handbook: Prescriptive Reading Inventory.* Monterey, Calif.: CTB/McGraw-Hill, 1972.

## INTERPRETATION OF TEST RESULTS

Proper interpretation of test scores can yield some important information for teachers. But test results must be approached cautiously since they can sometimes conceal as much as they reveal.

One problem is that tests only sample a small part of an individual's behavior, and at the extremes of a population distribution, scores may not reveal problems adequately. Test scores can be misleading for a variety of other reasons:

1. If timed, comprehension test scores will be lowered.

2. Objective-type tests for reading comprehension are imperfect since much guessing can occur. Though test norms include an average amount of guessing for normal readers, poor readers who tend to guess more may have their scores artificially inflated.

3. The probable error on even well-standardized tests can be large enough that small differences between scores of individuals may actually represent no difference at all.

4. Both teachers and machines can wrongly score tests. Errors in counting, problems in the use of keys, difficulty in following directions, inadequate use of tables of conversion, and problems in computation are almost inevitable and affect test results.

Because of such limitations, generalizations on the basis of test scores should ordinarily be avoided. Often more helpful than a determination of overall reading level are the kinds of errors made on a test since these are the weak spots around which the curriculum can be planned. Similarly, the range of scores is often more helpful than average (mean, median, or mode) scores because there may be no "average" children in the group.

Usually a more useful interpretive device than quantitative scores is the profile for individuals or a group that may result from testing. If several tests are used (a practice that is almost always better than using a single test), the several profiles may give a much more accurate picture of the individual or group than any set of figures.

One final caution to keep in mind is that norms of tests are based on general school populations. They fail to represent special groups such as particular regions, racial groups, or socioeconomic levels. Comparison of a low socioeconomic group with national norms is unfair inasmuch as the group will not have enjoyed the same advantages as are represented by national standards. In such situations tests should be used for diagnosis and specific help rather than for comparison. This same point holds true to a lesser degree for all groups.

For other useful readings on test result interpretation, see:

Farr, Roger. *Measurement and Evaluation of Reading.* New York: Harcourt Brace Jovanovich, 1970.

————. *Reading: What Can Be Measured?* Newark, Del.: International Reading Association, 1969.

Mehrens, William A., and Lehmann, Irvin J. *Standardized Tests in Education.* New York: Holt, Rinehart & Winston, 1969.

## KEEPING TESTS TO A MINIMUM

Almost all tests require reading, writing, or spelling, and sometimes all three. When pupils suffer from a disability in any aspect of language, they will score low on such tests, even though they actually may have learned a great deal in the content area being tested. They cannot demonstrate their knowledge because of a communication problem.

In such cases, therefore, teachers must be particularly conscious of the negative effects of testing. Many pupils will "freeze" whenever a test is even suggested because of the threat implicit in the testing situation to them as individuals. Oral tests can substitute sometimes for tests that embody printed or written communication; tests, as such, must be kept to a minimum. Grades must be based on many things other than test scores; otherwise, they are unfairly emphasizing only one aspect of behavior.

In this regard, teachers should strive to use only a few tests well rather than a large number of tests. And the tests used should not be administered in the space of a few days at one point in the semester. It is better to scatter them throughout the year, and incorporate results in curriculum change for that portion of the course. If the teaching of reading is one of the major objectives of the course, ordinarily a *single* reading test relatively early in the course for diagnostic and planning purposes and another comparable test at the end to determine gains are sufficient.

It is almost customary for teachers to reject testing, since it tends to subtract time from teaching. But with proper use of results tests can make teaching more, not less, efficient.

# GLOSSARY OF TERMS RELATING TO THE TEACHING OF READING

**Affix:** A unit (either a prefix or a suffix) put before or after a root to form a new word.

**Audience Reading:** The practice of having an individual or group read orally to a *listening* audience, that is, to an audience that is not following the text in a book.

**Audiometer:** A device for testing hearing ability for both acuity and pitch.

**Auditory Discrimination:** The act of hearing likenesses and differences in sounds.

**Basal Readers:** A series of books for teaching reading skills that increase gradually in difficulty from the readiness level through the sixth or eighth grade. They are usually accompanied by a teacher's guide, workbooks, and other special materials as learning aids.

**Basic Sight Vocabulary:** Common words in written material, recognized "at sight." Special lists, such as Dolch's Basic Sight Vocabulary, are designed to include the most common words found in printed English.

**Bibliotherapy:** The technique of using reading material to help children resolve their problems vicariously.

**Blend:** A combination of two or more phonemes in which each phoneme can be distinguished. The term applies most to consonant (*bl, cr*) rather than vowel combinations, which are more properly called "diphthongs."

**Choral Reading:** Oral reading in unison, occasionally with solo parts and harmonic arrangements.

**Closure:** The tendency to perceive an incomplete form as if it were complete.

**Compound Word:** A word made up of two or more smaller words (*afternoon, mother-in-law*).

**Concept of a Word:** The generalized but personal meaning that a word comes to have for a reader through his or her experiences connected with that word.

**Configuration (Clues):** The overall shape of a word—its length and distinctive features, especially the letters that are taller or that fall below the line in some part.

**Consonant:** A single letter (*b, c, d, f, g, h, j, k, l, m, n, p, q, r, s, t, v, x,* or *z*) representing a speech sound characterized by squeezing or stoppage at one or more points in the breath channel. *W* and *y*, often found acting as consonants, also sometimes serve as vowels and are therefore called "semivowels." Consonants may be referred to as initial, medial, or final, according to their position within the word. Some consonants (*c* and *g*) are called hard or soft, depending upon their sound. Some (*t, k, g*) may be silent in some words. See also **Blend** and **Digraph.**

**Consonant Substitution:** The act of using a known consonant sound in the initial or final position in combination with the sound of a known phonogram to form a new word. (When the *c* at the beginning of *car* is known and the word *boat* is known, the word *coat* can be analyzed by combining the known elements.)

**Context (Clues):** Words surrounding an unknown word that can be used to determine whether the new word (as analyzed) makes good sense in the sentence. Picture clues to a word are also a form of context clue. Both picture and verbal context clues lead to a type of expectancy for particular words.

**Contraction:** A shortened form for saying and writing two or three words which often occur together (I'm for I am).

**Control:** Any procedure in an experiment designed to eliminate the effect of a change in the factor under evaluation. Also, a population that does not have the experimental stimulus applied to it.

**Corrective Reading:** A program of help for children who have relatively mild reading difficulty, completely within the classroom situation.

**Correlation:** (Designated *r*, for product-moment correlation; *p-rho*, for the rank-difference method). This measure indicates the degree to which two separate sets of variables change together. If the correlation is 1.00, the prediction of one score from the other is exact; .80 is considered a high correlation. Predictive ability drops very rapidly from that point, though an *r* of .45 would indicate considerable relationship between two variables.

**Criterion-Referenced Test:** An inventory (a thorough measurement of a limited skill area) which samples desired student behaviors in a particular study area. Students are compared in their responses to expected behavior. Their mastery (or lack of it) of particular behaviors specified by an objective is measured. The scores indicate how much they know in terms of a specific behavioral objective.

**Critical Reading:** The act of evaluating carefully during reading, using the entire background of learning and experience.

**Developmental Reading:** Reading activities, primarily led by the teacher, designed to improve the reading level of the child. It also refers to the carefully planned sequence for the development of reading skills as the child becomes ready for each successive step.

**Digraph:** A combination of two or more letters, usually vowels or a vowel followed by *w*, which produces a single speech sound (as in *tail*, *goat*, *saw*; in consonants, *know*, *gnat*, *phonograph*).

**Diphthong:** A combination of two vowels that blend their sounds so that neither of the original long or short sounds is heard, but a combination of the two is produced (*oil*, *boy*, *how*). In some cases the consonant blends *ch*, *sh*, *th*, and *ph* may be consonant diphthongs (*phone*).

**Endings:** Additions to words, such as *s*, *es*, *ed*, *ied*, *ing*. Words made up of a word and an ending are called "variants" of the original word.

**Enrichment:** The provision of additional learning activities that extend or supplement the usual lesson. Ordinarily suggestions are found in the guide for the basal readers concerning such activities.

**Experience Story:** A summary story formulated by children under teacher guidance about an experience in which they have participated. The story is written on the board or a chart and used to develop reading skills.

**Eye Movements:** A series of alternating pauses and quick, jerky movements which the eyes perform when a person is reading. For the adult reader each pause will take in at least one word and is longer in time than the movement itself.

**Eye-Voice Span:** In oral reading, the distance between the place the eyes are looking and the words the voice is pronouncing. The span is usually several words for most adult readers.

**Fixations:** The pauses that occur in the eye movements during reading, when the reader focuses on the words. See **Eye Movements.**

**Flash Cards:** Large cards for a group, or smaller cards for individual use, with words printed on them to present new words, review old words, and increase speed of recognition.

**Frequency Distribution:** A tabulation showing the number of scores that occur within a certain interval, arranged in ascending order of scores.

**Frustration Level:** The level at which reading becomes too difficult for the child to realize progress. Excessive errors (more than one word in every running twenty), poor comprehension, and emotional tension are signs it has been reached.

**Functional Reading:** Reading in which the primary purpose is to gain information or understanding; reading to learn.

**Grouping:** Placing children together by achievement level, special needs, interests, or goals for more efficient learning.

**Guided Reading:** Reading (usually from the basal reader) for which the teacher provides the purpose. The children read silently, then discuss the answer to a question posed, and perhaps read orally.

**Hearing Vocabulary:** The words a child or adult understands when he or she hears them. The ability to speak, read, or write the same words is not necessary. It may also be referred to as "listening vocabulary."

**Heterogeneous (Grouping):** A population distribution reflecting a wide range of variability.

**Homogeneous (Grouping):** A population that has the characteristic of being the same in regard to one or more variables.

**Homograph:** A word with the same written form but several different meanings and sounds determined by the context (*lead, read, desert*).

**Homonyms:** Words that sound alike, though they may be spelled either alike or differently, and which have different meanings (*steak, stake*).

**Independent Level:** The level of reading at which the material is sufficiently easy so that the child may proceed on his or her own without help and gain pleasure. The independent reading level is assumed to be the level at which there is less than one unknown word for every one hundred running words.

**Individualized Reading:** In the past, "free reading" or "independent reading" for pleasure, practice, or information, but now, a method of teaching developmental reading using trade books instead of basal readers. Children seek out and select their own books, pace themselves, and have individual conferences with the teacher.

**Inflectional Ending:** A suffix which indicates number, tense, possession, comparison, present participle, or third person singular. See **Endings.**

**Informal Reading Inventory:** A test of reading ability which uses graded paragraphs, usually from a basal series, rather than a prepared copy in the usual test form. The child reads up through the series to the frustration level while the teacher notes errors and checks comprehension.

**Inner Speech:** Reading silently, but still "hearing" the words being pronounced as they are read. It is often accompanied by subvocal movements of the voice mechanism.

**Instructional Level:** The reading level at which material may be most efficiently taught. This is determined by the error rate, which is usually two or three percent (out of every hundred words, two or three are unknown).

**Intelligence Quotient (IQ):** A measure of mental development, with a figure of 100 as the population mean. The IQ is the mental age divided by the chronological age and multiplied by one hundred.

**Joplin Plan:** A system of interclass grouping, whereby children of all ages who are reading at the same level are grouped together during the reading period for instruction. The plan is so named because it was popularized in Joplin, Missouri.

**Kinesthetic (Method):** A method of teaching reading that adds the tracing of large word forms with the fingers to the ordinary visual and auditory approach. It is used mainly in remedial reading.

**Lateral (or Hemispheric) Dominance:** The control that one side of the brain exercises over hand, eye, and foot movements on the opposite side. If a person is right handed, it is the left hemisphere of the brain that controls. Consistency in direction seems to be important in determining those children who will exhibit fewer reversals in learning to read.

**Left-Right Direction:** The arbitrary direction in which English is read.

**Line Graph:** A diagrammatic representation of performance over a period of time, often used in test profiles and in student progress charts. Time is usually shown on the horizontal axis and performance on the vertical axis.

**Location Skills:** The ability to find entries in a reference work easily and quickly. Alphabetizing, use of guide words, skimming, and so forth are essential components.

**Matched Groups:** In an experiment, two groups equated on specific variables such as intelligence, age, or socioeconomic status. One group is presented with the experimental variable and the other group (the control group) is not; results are then compared.

**Mental Age:** Age of mental development of an individual, usually expressed in months or years and months, as compared to the standardization group on an intelligence test.

**Metaphor:** A word which in ordinary usage signifies one kind of thing, quality, or action as applied to another without express indication of a relationship between them (Richard the Lionhearted). A simile without the words *as* or *like*.

**Morpheme:** A meaningful portion of a word, such as a prefix, suffix, root, or inflectional ending.

**Normal Curve:** A symmetrical, bell-shaped curve, depicting a normal (expected) distribution of scores.

**Overlapping:** The extent to which scores of one distribution are the same as those of another distribution. It is usually expressed as a percentage of one set exceeding the mean of another set.

**Pacing:** Allowing the child to set her or his own speed in reading, even if this means doing very little reading. The technique is associated primarily with the individualized reading method.

**Paraphrasing:** Restating a writer's thoughts in one's own words by way of summarizing.

**Percentile:** A point along a scale of scores in a distribution below which a given percent of the scores occur. (Twenty percent of the scores are below the twentieth percentile.)

**Phoneme:** The smallest unit of speech sound. It may be represented by one or several letters (*a, eigh*).

**Phonetics:** The scientific study of speech sounds, including pronunciation, action of the speech mechanism, and sound symbolization.

**Phonics:** The study of the speech equivalents of printed symbols, and their use in pronouncing written words; also, the application of phonetics to reading and spelling.

**Phonogram:** A written unit which represents a phoneme. One kind of phonogram is sometimes known as the "word family" (*ake, ill, at,* etc.).

**Population:** Any group of individuals who are alike in at least one specific way (all fifth-grade pupils in a school; all high school students enrolled in American history in a district).

**Prefix:** A meaningful beginning portion of a word which modifies the meaning of the root word to which it is attached.

**Preprimer:** A paperbound booklet presenting the first stories in a series of basal readers, for use immediately following the readiness materials. There are usually three of them is a set, running about fifty pages in length, with large pictures, few words, and much repetition.

**Primer:** Literally means "first book," but is now preceded by the readiness book or books and the preprimers in a basal series. It is ordinarily the first clothbound book, approximately 150 pages in length, and maintains the vocabulary of the preprimers as well as adding new words.

**Profile:** A line graph which pictures the relative position of an individual or group with respect to each of several scores or traits. Variation of different scores and the general trend are revealed.

**Random Sample:** A population selected from a larger group in a purely random manner, not according to any preset characteristics (as taking every twentieth name from a list).

**Range:** The distance in score values between the highest and lowest in a distribution.

**Rapport:** A comfortable relationship of mutual confidence between people.

**Rate of Comprehension:** Speed of reading with understanding, as contrasted to simple rate of reading.

**Raw Score:** The original score obtained by measurement (as number of items correct on a test).

**Readability:** Difficulty (and sometimes interest) level of reading material, often obtained through the use of a formula.

**Reading:** The meaningful interpretation of written symbols in which the reader brings his or her previous experiences with language symbols to bear upon the new organization of these symbols provided by the writer.

**Reading Capacity:** The level of potential in reading, ordinarily determined through intelligence or listening comprehension tests.

**Reading Disability:** A situation in which a child's reading level is significantly (usually over one year) below his or her capacity level.

**Reading Grade:** The most common score given by reading tests, expressed in years and tenths of years, corresponding to school grade placement. (A score of 5.6 means fifth grade sixth month placement on the distribution since ten months corresponds to a normal school year and is easily handled statistically.)

**Reading Readiness.** The general stage of developmental maturity at which the child can learn to read easily, effectively, and efficiently without much personal disturbance. The term may be used to signify ability to begin each succeeding stage of reading development as well as for beginning reading.

**Reading Retardation:** A situation in which a child is reading below grade level. Contrasted with **Reading Disability.**

**Reading Vocabulary:** The words which a child can read and understand.

**Recognition Span:** The amount seen in an average fixation, usually expressed in number of words.

**Recreational Reading:** Reading for fun as contrasted with reading for utilitarian purposes.

**Regression:** Backward movement of the eyes along the line of print or back up the page in order to get a second look.

**Related Practice:** Usually, review of skills or vocabulary presented previously in the basal reader lesson. Use of a workbook designed to correlate with a basal reader is an example.

**Reliability:** The extent to which a test will yield the same score or nearly the same score on successive trials, expressed as a correlation coefficient.

**Remedial Reading:** Help given to reading disability cases either individually or in small groups by a specially prepared teacher outside the regular classroom.

**Rereading:** Usually, oral reading of a basal story after silent reading has been completed to prove a point raised in discussion, dramatize the story, evaluate word recognition, and so forth.

**Return Sweep:** The eye movement back to the left margin and one line further down the page after completion of a line of reading in a connected paragraph. It is probably the most difficult eye movement to learn in the reading process.

**Reversals:** A tendency (especially among immature readers) to read from right-to-left instead of left-to-right (*saw* for *was, no* for *on*).

**Root Word:** A basic word in English, derived mainly from Latin or Greek, to which prefixes and suffixes may be added.

**Sample:** A group drawn from a larger population to represent that population. See **Random Sample.**

**Schwa:** The vowel sound in an unaccented syllable in English that is neither short nor long. It is diacritically marked as ə.

**Seeking:** A technique of teaching reading by giving a child the opportunity to explore a wide variety of reading activities and materials.

**Self-Selection:** The technique used in individualized reading of allowing a child to exercise his or her own preference in choosing books.

**Semantics:** The scientific study of meanings, particularly the meanings of words.

**Simile:** A comparison between two essentially different items, expressed by the word *as* or *like* (busy as a bee).

**Skimming:** Looking rapidly through printed material for a specific reference (not reading).

**SQ3R Formula:** A study method developed by Francis P. Robinson consisting of (1) *S*urveying the material, (2) making a *Q*uestion from each section heading, (3) *R*eading with the question in mind, (4) *R*eciting the answer to yourself, and (5) *R*eviewing at suitable intervals.

**Stanine:** A point measured along the distribution of scores below which a given one-tenth of the scores occurs. The range is from one ⁱ nine, one being the low end of the distribution.

**Structural Analysis:** Analysis of words in terms of their morphemes or meaning units. By contrast phonic analysis takes words apart or puts them together on the basis of sound. The two methods are often used together in the reading program.

**Suffix:** A meaningful ending portion of a word which modifies the meaning of the root word to which it is attached.

**Supplementary Reading:** Additional sets of readers to the basal reader at a similar or easier reading level. The teacher provides guidance in their use, but not to the same degree as with the basal reader.

**Syllable:** A unit of speech sound containing one vowel sound. It is unbroken and forms either a whole or part of a word.

**Synonym:** A word meaning almost the same as another word. (NOTE: There are very few words which mean *exactly* the same thing.)

**Tachistoscope:** A mechanical device that flashes an image for a very short period of time, used as an aid in increasing reading speed. Most of these devices project the image and employ a shutter of some type to control the length of time of projection.

**Teacher's Manual:** A guidebook showing how best to use a particular piece of reading material in the classroom. All basal readers, as well as many other books and kits, have this feature.

**Team Teaching:** A form of administrative grouping where two or four classrooms are put together (tearing the dividing walls down, in some cases), and a "team" of teachers shares teaching duties, conferring on plans and problems, and so forth.

**Validity:** The degree to which a test measures what it has been devised to measure, expressed by a correlation coefficient.

**Variable:** Any condition in an experimental situation which may affect the observations made. The term "independent variable" refers to the thing observed or measured; the term "dependent variable" to the responses.

**Visual Discrimination:** The ability to see likenesses and differences in shape and form, especially in letters and words.

**Vocabulary Control:** Careful limitation of words introduced (especially in basal readers and some trade books) to conform to word lists or other prestructured bases. For example, the vocabulary in most present-day first-grade basal reading programs is between 350 to 500 of the most common words in English.

**Vocabulary Lists:** Compilations of words, based on word count research, which indicate the most commonly used words in reading and writing. In general, stories are written first and then checked against such lists.

**Vowel:** The speech sounds (*a, e, i, o,* and *u*) produced without obstructing the breath, with the vocal cavities open and formed for resonance. *Y* and *w* are *semivowels*. Each of these single vowels may have a long sound, a short sound, the schwa sound, or a sound modified by *r* or *l*.

**Word Analysis:** The study of a word by phonic analysis and/or structural analysis to determine its identity. Also called "word attack."

**Word-by-Word Reading:** Reading very slowly with a hesitation between each word. Such reading usually indicates poor word recognition or insecurity.

**Word-Form (Clues):** See **Configuration (Clues).**

**Word Recognition:** The identification of a word in print as a word previously known in one's speech or listening vocabulary.

**Workbook:** A book designed as a reinforcing and skill-developing tool, usually used as related reading, especially with basal readers. It is generally designed so a child can mark in it.

**Work-type Reading:** Functional reading to find information; synonymous with "study-type reading" or exercises in the "work-study skills."

# BIBLIOGRAPHY

Below is a list of books, arranged by topic, which can be used with profit to expand on points made in this book. The references are abbreviated here. For the complete publication data and the particular subtopic to which the readings are most applicable, turn to the page listed after the title.

## READING DEVELOPMENT

Allen, "The Right to Read," 4.
Aukerman, *Reading in the Secondary School Classroom*, 9.
Bamman, *Fundamentals of Basic Reading Instruction*, 8.
Carrillo, *Informal Reading Readiness Experiences*, 6.
Clymer, "What Is Reading," 3.
Dallmann, *The Teaching of Reading*, 3, 8.
Duggins, *Teaching Reading for Human Values in High School*, 9.
Durkin, *Teaching Them to Read*, 4.
Ekwall, *Locating and Correcting Reading Difficulties*, 8.
Gray, "The Major Aspects of Reading," 3.
Hafner, *Patterns of Teaching Reading in the Elementary School*, 8.
Miller, *The First R*, 6.
Monroe, *Foundations for Reading*, 6.
Otto, *Focused Reading Instruction*, 11.
Otto and Askov, *Rationale and Guidelines*, 11.
*Prescriptive Reading Inventory* and *Interpretive Handbook*, 11.
*Report of the National Committee on Reading*, 5.
Spache, E., *Reading Activities for Child Involvement*, 11.
Strang, *The Improvement of Reading*, 5.

## INSTRUCTIONAL METHODS

Allen, *Language Experiences in Reading*, 16.
Anderson, *The Psychology of Teaching Reading*, 18.

Ashton-Warner, *Teacher*, 16.
Barbe, *Educator's Guide to Personalized Reading Instruction*, 26.
Burton, *Reading in Child Development*, 20.
Buswell, *Non-Oral Reading*, 21.
Carrillo, "The Language-Experience Approach to the Teaching of Reading," 16.
Durrell, *Durrell Analysis of Reading Difficulty*, 8.
Fernald, *Remedial Techniques in the Basic School Subjects*, 23.
Fries, *Linguistics and Reading*, 20.
Fry, *Reading Instruction for Classroom and Clinic*, 31.
Gans, *Guiding Children's Reading Through Experiences*, 16.
Godfrey, *Individualizing with Learning Station Themes*, 28.
———, *Individualizing Through Learning Stations*, 28.
Gray, *On Their Own in Reading*, 31.
Hafner, *Patterns of Teaching Reading in the Elementary School*, 18.
Harris, *How to Increase Reading Ability*, 33.
Heilman, *Phonics in Proper Perspective*, 31.
Herrick, *Using Experience Charts with Children*, 16.
Hunt, "Individualized Reading," 26.
———, "The Key to the Conference Lies in Questioning," 26.
Lee, *Learning to Read Through Experience*, 16.
McCracken, G., "New Castle Reading Experiment," 22.
———, "The Value of the Correlated Visual Image," 22.
McCracken, R., *Reading Is Only the Tiger's Tail*, 26.
McDade, "Essentials of Non-Oral Beginning Reading," 21.
Miller, *The First R*, 26.
Olson, "Reading as a Function of Total Growth," 27.
Smith, F., *Understanding Reading*, 20.
Smith, N., *American Reading Instruction*, 18.
Spache, G., *Reading in the Elementary School*, 31.
Spache, G. and E., *Toward Better Reading*, 31.
Strang, *Making Better Readers*, 20.
Tinker, *Teaching Elementary Reading*, 33.
Veatch, *Individualizing Your Reading*, 27.
———, *Reading in the Elementary School*, 27.
Zintz, *The Reading Process*, 18.

## THE IMPROVEMENT OF READING SKILLS

Aukerman, *Reading in the Secondary School Classroom*, 58.
Bamman, *Fundamentals of Basic Reading Instruction*, 64.
Chall, *Learning to Read*, 50.
Dallmann, *The Teaching of Reading*, 36, 37, 51, 58.
Duffy, *How to Teach Reading Systematically*, 51.

## INTERESTS AND ATTITUDES

McCracken, R., *Reading Is Only the Tiger's Tail*, 73.
Sax, *Principles of Educational Measurement and Evaluation*, 70.
Shaw, *Scales for the Measurement of Attitude*, 70.
Spache, *Good Reading for Poor Readers*, 69.
————, *Reading Activities for Child Involvement*, 73.
Strang, *Diagnostic Teaching of Reading*, 67, 70.
————, *The Improvement of Reading*, 70.
Witty, *Reading in Modern Education*, 67.

## READING DISABILITY AND RETARDATION: KINDS, CAUSES, AND REMEDIATION

Austin, *Reading Evaluation*, 83, 84, 88.
Bamman, *Fundamentals of Basic Reading Instruction*, 95.
Barbe, "Instructional Causes of Poor Reading," 91.
Bond, *Reading Difficulties*, 77, 83, 88.
Carrillo, "Reactions For and Against the Special Remedial Reading Class," 80.
————, "The Relation of Certain Environmental and Developmental Factors to Reading Ability in Children," 89.
Carter, *Diagnosis and Treatment of the Disabled Reader*, 85.
Dallmann, Martha, *The Teaching of Reading*, 95.
Department of Elementary School Principals, *Parents and the Schools*, 95.
Ekwall, *Psychological Factors in the Teaching of Reading*, 86, 88, 90.
Freshour, "Beginning Reading," 95.
Froelich, *Guidance Testing*, 90.
Fry, *Reading Instruction for Classroom and Clinic*, 88.
*A Graded List of Books for School Libraries*, 100.
Grant, *Parents and Teachers as Partners*, 95.
Greene, *Reading*, 91.
Guszak, *Diagnostic Reading Instruction in the Elementary School*, 86.
Harris, *How to Increase Reading Ability*, 100.
Heilman, *Principles and Practices of Teaching Reading*, 91.
Hymes, *Effective Home-School Relations*, 95.
Kennedy, *Classroom Approaches to Remedial Reading*, 83.
Kottmeyer, *Teacher's Guide for Remedial Reading*, 80.
Kough, *Identifying Children with Special Needs*, 83.
Langdon, *Helping Parents Understand Their Child's School*, 95.
Lee, "San Diego City Schools," 80.
*The Reading Teacher*, 80.
Robinson, *Reading Instruction in Various Patterns of Grouping*, 78.
Schubert, *Improving the Reading Program*, 84, 97.
Sheldon, "Relation of Parents, Home, and Certain Developmental Characteristics to Children's Reading Ability," 89.

## TEXTBOOK SELECTION

## TESTING

# INDEX